Vanna's
Afghans A to Z

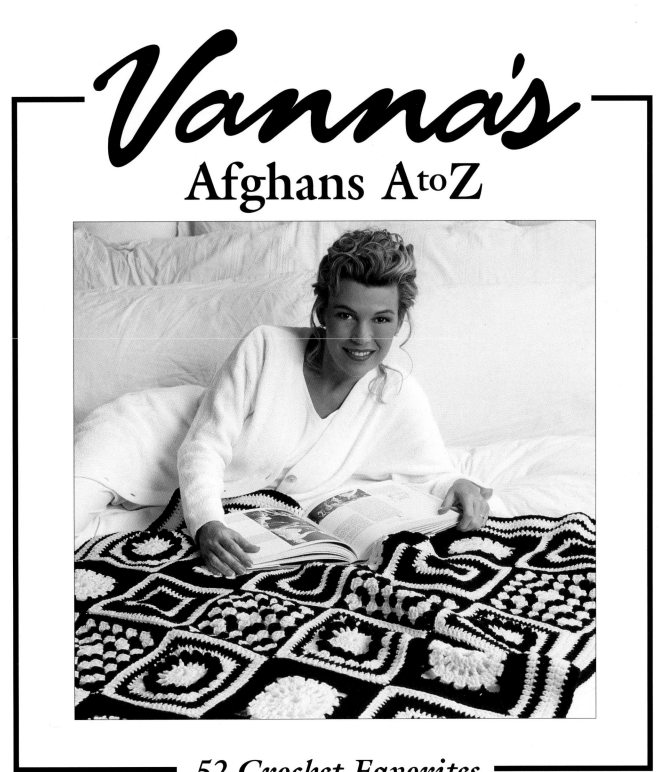

52 Crochet Favorites

©1994 by Oxmoor House, Inc.
Book Division of Southern Progress Corporation
P.O. Box 2463, Birmingham, Alabama 35201

Published by Oxmoor House, Inc., and Leisure Arts, Inc.

Library of Congress Catalog Number: 94-69236
Hardcover ISBN: 0-8487-1435-0
Softcover ISBN: 0-8487-1476-8
Manufactured in the United States of America
Second Printing 1995

Editor-in-Chief: Nancy J. Fitzpatrick
Senior Crafts Editor: Susan Ramey Wright
Senior Editor, Editorial Services: Olivia Kindig Wells
Art Director: James Boone

Vanna's Afghans A to Z: 52 Crochet Favorites

Editor: Catherine S. Corbett
Contributing Editors: Carol Cook Hagood, Margaret Allen Price,
    Shannon L. Sexton
Editorial Assistant: Janica Lynn York
Copy Editor: L. Amanda Owens
Copy Assistant: Jennifer K. Mathews
Senior Photographer: John O'Hagan
Photographer: Ralph Anderson
Photostylist: Katie Stoddard
Designer: Mary Grace Wright
Production and Distribution Director: Phillip Lee
Production Manager: Gail Morris
Associate Production Manager: Theresa L. Beste
Production Assistant: Marianne Jordan
Artist: Kelly Davis
Senior Production Designer: Larry Hunter
Publishing Systems Administrator: Rick Tucker

This book is dedicated with love to my grandmother Albertene Nicholas. Not only did she enjoy crocheting, but she also taught me how to do my first chain stitch!

Vanna White and her son, Nicholas

Table of Contents

Introduction

Glittering and glamorous—that's how you may think of my life-style.

In the dozen years since I became the hostess of television's "Wheel of Fortune," I've appeared on hundreds of shows, demonstrating incredible prizes and encouraging contestants as they reach to make a dream come true—all the while modeling fabulous fashions.

But there's another part of my life on "Wheel" that you have never seen. Between shows (we tape five in a day of filming) or during free moments while prospective contestants are being interviewed, I have something else that fills my time.

I have a backstage passion that may surprise you: I crochet! Over the years, crocheting has become my favorite hobby.

Since 1983, when a hairdresser on the set taught me several stitches to add to the basic chain stitch my grandmother had taught me, I've been stitching away at every opportunity.

An unusual diversion for a TV personality? Not really when you think of all the benefits crocheting offers. First of all, crochet is so *portable*. It's just right to pass the time while waiting for appointments or traveling. I never board a plane without a project! Also, crochet is *relaxing*—a guaranteed stress-reliever for a busy life-style. And what's more, crochet is *rewarding*. It repays me with something really beautiful to show for my time.

In fact, I've made more than 70 afghans as gifts for Pat Sajak, Merv Griffin, and many other friends.

No matter who I want to surprise, I think that a handmade gift is the best present possible. Everyone loves afghans and responds to their wonderful, inviting colors and textures. By choosing a pattern that suits a friend and stitching it up in his or her favorite colors, I can create a one-of-a-kind gift.

When David Blumenthal, vice president of Lion Brand Yarns, learned of my love of crochet, he asked me to serve as a spokesperson for the craft, "living proof" that people of any age can find crocheting to be a terrific hobby.

With this book, I continue the role of introducing friends and fans to the pleasures of crochet. The editors at Oxmoor House, Leisure Arts, Lion Brand Yarns, and I have worked together to present 52 beautiful designs—two for every letter of the alphabet. (You know how I love letters!) Among them you will find designs for every taste and skill level. If you're a beginner, take time to carefully study the General Directions at the back of the book.

Let me recommend some easy afghans you'll enjoy:

• *Vanna's Choice* (page 112) is a pattern I have used to make so many of my gift afghans. This afghan pattern is easy to learn. It's made almost entirely with simple double crochet stitch, worked plain or in an easy mesh.

• Other afghans just right for beginners are *X Marks the Spot* (page 122) and *Granny's Delight* (page 41).

In the pages that follow, see how these and the dozens of other designs worked in contemporary colors and timeless patterns give crochet a fresh, new feel. In some of the

photos, you're invited to come with me right into my home and see how crochet finds its place in my world and in my life—as a television personality and as a wife and a mother. I hope you will be inspired to choose your favorite patterns, pick up a hook, and join me in the fun of crochet!

A August Morning

August Morning

*Take time to relax with the morning news, a cup
of herbal tea—my favorite—and an afghan
as soft as a summer breeze.*

Finished Size

Approximately 53" x 84"

Materials

Lion Brand Keepsake Sayelle* worsted-weight yarn (6 oz., 312-yd. skein): 9 Black #153; 6 Pine #182; 2 Lilac #143; 1 each Goldenrod #187, Fuchsia #186, Robin Blue #107, Purple #147, Peach #184

Size H crochet hook or size to obtain gauge

Gauge

Square = 3½"

Directions

Square: Make 360 total. Make 60 ea using Lilac, Goldenrod, Fuchsia, Robin Blue, Purple, and Peach for Flowers. Use Pine for Leaves and Black for Border.

Flower (WS): Ch 4, join with sl st to form a ring, ch 3, work 3 dc in ring, drop lp from hook, insert hook in top of beg ch-3, pick up dropped lp and pull through (beg popcorn made), ch 3, [work 4 dc in ring, drop lp from hook, insert hook in first st of 4-dc grp, pick up dropped lp and pull through

(popcorn made), ch 3] 3 times, sl st in top of beg popcorn = 4 popcorns around. Fasten off.

Leaves: With RS facing, join Pine with sl st in any ch-3 sp, ch 3 (for first dc), (2 dc, ch 3, 3 dc) in same sp, ch 1, * (3 dc, ch 3, 3 dc) in next ch-3 sp, ch 1, rep from * around, sl st in top of beg ch-3 = 24 dc around. Fasten off.

Border: With RS facing, join Black with sl st in any corner ch-3 sp, ch 3 (for first dc), (3 dc, ch 3, 3 dc) in same sp, ch 1, 3 dc in next ch-1 sp, * (3 dc, ch 3, 3 dc) in next corner ch-3 sp, ch 1, 3 dc in next ch-1 sp, ch 1, rep from * around, sl st in top of beg ch-3 = 36 dc around. Fasten off.

Assembly: With Black, whipstitch squares together through back loops only to make 24 strips of 15 squares each, using matching flower colors in each strip. Whipstitch strips together in the following sequence: * Lilac, Goldenrod, Fuchsia, Robin Blue, Peach, Purple, rep from * 3 times more.

Border: Join Black with sl st in any corner, ch 1, * (2 sc, ch 1, 2 sc) in same corner, sc evenly across to next corner, rep from * around, sl st in first sc. Fasten off.

A
American Beauty

American Beauty

Rows of red, white, and blue—how patriotic!
With quick-stitch stripes and simple shells, it's
a colorful way to say "I love America."

Finished Size

Approximately 47" x 64"

Materials

Lion Brand Keepsake Sayelle* worsted-weight yarn (6 oz., 312-yd. skein): 3 Scarlet #113 (MC); 3 each Cream #098 (A), Navy #111 (B)
Size H crochet hook or size to obtain gauge

Gauge

6 sts and 5 rows in pat = 2"

Directions

Stripe Sequence: Work in pat as specified below, changing colors in the foll sequence: 2 rows MC, 2 rows A, 2 rows B, 1 row MC, (1 row B, 1 row A, 1 row MC) twice, * 2 rows B, 2 rows A, 3 rows MC, 2 rows A, 2 rows B, 1 row MC, (1 row B, 1 row A, 1 row MC) twice, rep from * 4 times more, 2 rows B, 2 rows A, 2 rows MC.

Afghan: Ch 194 loosely.
Row 1 (RS): Dc in 4th ch from hook and in ea rem ch across, turn = 192 dc across.
Row 2: Ch 1, sc in first dc and in ea st across, turn.
Row 3: Ch 3 (for first dc), dc in next sc and in ea sc across, turn.
Rows 4–6: Rep Rows 2 and 3 once, then rep Row 2 once more.

Row 7: Ch 3 (for first dc), sk next 2 sc, 5 dc in next st (shell made), * sk next 4 sc, shell in next sc, rep from * across to last 3 sc, sk next 2 sc, dc in last sc, turn = 38 shells across.
Row 8: Ch 3 (for first dc), 2 dc in same st, work (shell in sp bet next 2 shells) across to last shell, sk last shell, 3 dc in last dc, turn = 37 shells across.
Row 9: Ch 3 (for first dc), work (shell in center dc of next shell 2 rows below) across, dc in last dc on prev row, turn = 38 shells across.
Row 10: Ch 3 (for first dc), 2 dc in same st, (shell in center dc of next shell 2 rows below) across, 3 dc in last dc on prev row, turn = 37 shells across.
Rows 11–13: Rep Rows 9 and 10 once, then rep Row 9 once more.
Row 14: Ch 1, sc in first dc and in ea dc across, turn = 192 sc across.
Row 15: Ch 3 (for first dc), dc in next sc and in ea sc across, turn.
Row 16: Ch 1, sc in first dc and in ea dc across, turn.
Rows 17–24: Rep Rows 15 and 16, 4 times.
Rows 25–109: Rep Rows 7–24, 4 times, then rep Rows 7–19 once more. Do not fasten off.

Border: With RS facing and MC, ch 3 (for first dc), * dc evenly across to next corner of afghan, 3 dc in corner, rep from * around, sl st in top of beg ch-3. Fasten off.

B

Blanket
Buddies

Blanket Buddies

It's fun to stitch a pair of snuggly friends.
Wrap your little one in love with
a cozy bear or bunny.

Finished Size

Approximately 40" square

Materials

Lion Brand Keepsake Sayelle* worsted-weight yarn (6 oz., 312-yd. skein): *For bear:* 5 Cocoa Brown #123 (MC), 1 Black #153. *For bunny:* 6 Lilac #143 (MC), 1 White #100

Sizes H and I crochet hooks or size to obtain gauge

Stuffing

2 (¾"-diameter) wiggle eyes for each afghan

Sewing thread

Gauge

Blanket: Rnds 1–3 = 4" square with size H hook

Directions

Blanket: With size H hook and MC, ch 3, join with sl st to form a ring.

Rnd 1 (RS): Ch 7 (for first dc and ch 4), (3 dc in ring, ch 4) 3 times, 2 dc in ring, sl st in 3rd ch of beg ch-7 = 12 dc around.

Rnd 2: Sl st into first ch-4 sp, ch 3 (for first dc), (dc, ch 4, 2 dc) in same sp, dc in ea of next 3 dc, * (2 dc, ch 4, 2 dc) in next ch-4 sp, dc in ea of next 3 dc, rep from * around, sl st in top of beg ch-3 = 28 dc around.

Rnds 3–38: Sl st in next dc and in first ch-4 sp, ch 3 (for first dc), (dc, ch 4, 2 dc) in same sp, * dc in ea dc to next ch-4 sp, (2 dc, ch 4, 2 dc) in ch-4 sp, rep from * around, sl st in top of beg ch-3 = 604 dc around after Rnd 38. Fasten off.

Hood: **Row 1** (RS): With size H hook and MC, ch 4, 4 dc in 4th ch from hook, turn = 5 dc across.

Row 2 (WS): Ch 3 (for first dc), dc in same st, dc in ea dc across to last st, 2 dc in last st, turn = 7 dc across.

Row 3: Ch 3 (for first dc), 2 dc in same st, dc in ea dc across to last st, 3 dc in last st, turn = 11 dc across.

Rows 4–17: Rep Rows 2 and 3 alternately, turn = 53 dc across after Row 17.

Row 18 (fold row): Ch 3 (for first dc), (yo and pull up a lp in ft lp only of next dc, yo and pull through 2 lps on hook) 3 times, yo and pull through all 4 lps on hook (dc dec over 3 sts made), dc in ea dc across to last 4 dc, dc dec over next 3 sts, dc in last st, turn = 49 dc across.

Row 19: Ch 3 (for first dc), (yo and pull up a lp in next dc, yo and pull through 2 lps on hook) twice, yo and pull through all 3 lps on hook (dc dec over 2 sts made), dc in ea dc across to last 3 dc, dc dec over next 2 sts, dc in last st, turn = 47 dc across.

Row 20: Ch 3 (for first dc), dc dec over 3 sts, dc in ea dc across to last 4 dc, dc dec over 3 sts, dc in last st, turn = 43 dc across.

Row 21: Ch 3 (for first dc), dc dec over 2 sts, dc in ea dc across to last 3 dc, dc dec over next 2 sts, dc in last st, turn = 41 dc across.

Rows 22–33: Rep Rows 20 and 21 alternately, turn = 5 dc across after Row 33.

Row 34: Ch 2, (yo and pull up a lp in next dc, yo and pull through 2 lps on hook) 4 times, yo and pull through all 5 lps on hook. Fasten off.

Bear Muzzle: With size H hook and MC, ch 3, join with sl st to form a ring.

Rnd 1 (RS): Ch 1, 6 sc in ring, sl st in first sc.

Rnd 2: Ch 1, 2 sc in same st and in ea st around, sl st in first sc = 12 sc around.

Rnd 3: Ch 1, sc in same st, 2 sc in next sc, (sc in next sc, 2 sc in next sc) around, sl st in first sc = 18 sc around.

Rnd 4: Ch 1, sc in same st, sc in next sc, 2 sc in next sc, (sc in ea of next 2 sc, 2 sc in next sc) around, sl st in first sc = 24 sc around.

Rnd 5: Ch 1, sc in same st and in ea of next 2 sc, 2 sc in next sc, (sc in ea of next 3 sc, 2 sc in next sc) around, sl st in first sc = 30 sc around.

Rnd 6: Ch 1, sc in same st and in ea of next 3 sc, 2 sc in next sc, (sc in ea of next 4 sc, 2 sc in next sc) around, sl st in first sc = 36 sc around.

continued on page 14

continued from page 13

Rnd 7: Ch 1, sc in same st and in ea of next 4 sc, 2 sc in next sc, (sc in ea of next 5 sc, 2 sc in next sc) around, sl st in first sc = 42 sc around.

Rnd 8: Ch 1, sc in same st and in ea sc around, sl st in first sc. Fasten off, leaving a tail for sewing.

***Bear Nose:* Rnd 1:** With size H hook and Black, ch 4 loosely, 4 sc in 2nd ch from hook, sc in next ch, 4 sc in last ch, sc in free lp of next ch, join with sl st in first sc = 10 sc around.

Rnd 2: Ch 1, sc in same st and in ea sc around, sl st in first sc. Fasten off, leaving a tail for sewing.

Bear Ear (make 2): **Back:** With size I hook and MC, ch 3, join with sl st to form a ring.

Rnd 1 (RS): Ch 1, 6 sc in ring, sl st in first sc.

Rnds 2–5: Rep Rnds 2–5 as for bear muzzle. Fasten off after last rnd.

Front: Rep Rnds 1–5 as for ear back. Do not fasten off after last rnd.

Joining Rnd: With wrong sides facing, holding ear front and back tog, and working through both layers, ch 1, sc in ea st around, sl st in first sc. Fasten off, leaving a tail for sewing.

Bear Assembly: Referring to photo, stitch nose to muzzle and embroider mouth with Black. With wrong sides facing, fold hood in half along Row 18. Working through top layer only, stitch muzzle to hood, stuffing lightly before closing. Stitch ears and wiggle eyes in place on hood.

***Bunny Muzzle:* Rnd 1** (RS): With size H hook and MC, ch 14 loosely, work 2 dc in 4th ch from hook, dc in ea of next 8 ch, 2 dc in next ch, 3 dc in last ch, working across opposite side of foundation ch, 2 dc in next ch, dc in ea of next 8 ch, 2 dc in ea of next 2 ch, sl st in top of beg ch = 30 sts around.

Rnd 2: Ch 1, sc in same st, hdc in next st, 2 dc in next st, 2 tr in next st, 2 dc in next st, hdc in next st, sc in ea of next 2 sts, hdc in next st, 2 dc in next st, 2 tr in next st, 2 dc in next st, hdc in next st, sc in next st, 3 sc in next st, sc in ea of next 14 sts, 3 sc in last st, sl st in first sc = 40 sts around.

Rnd 3: Ch 1, sc in same st and in ea of next 2 sts, 2 hdc in next st, 2 dc in ea of next 3 sts, hdc in next st, sc in ea of next 4 sts, hdc in next st, 2 dc in ea of next 3 sts, 2 hdc in next st, sc in ea rem st around, sl st in first sc. Fasten off, leaving a tail for sewing.

Bunny Ear (make 2): **Front: Row 1** (RS): With size I hook and White, ch 25 loosely, sc in 2nd ch from hook and in ea rem ch across, 3 sc in last ch, working across opposite side of foundation ch, sc in ea of 23 ch, turn = 49 sc around.

Row 2: Ch 1, sc in ea of next 24 sc, 3 sc in next sc, sc in ea rem sc. Fasten off.

Back: With size I hook and MC, rep Rows 1 and 2 as for ear front. Do not fasten off after last rnd.

Joining Rnd: With wrong sides facing, holding ear front and back tog, and working through both layers, ch 1, sc in ea st around (inc as needed to keep work flat), sl st in first sc. Fasten off, leaving a tail for sewing.

Bunny Assembly: Referring to photo, embroider nose and mouth on muzzle with White. With wrong sides facing, fold hood in half along Row 18. Working through top layer only, stitch muzzle to hood, stuffing lightly before closing. Stitch ears and wiggle eyes in place on hood.

Blanket Assembly and Border: Work border around edge of each blanket as follows: Pin hood right side up to 1 corner on wrong side of Blanket. With hood facing and working through all layers, use size H hook to join MC with sl st in end of Row 17 on hood, ch 1, sc evenly around blanket, working 4 sc in ea corner, sl st in first sc. Fasten off.

B
Buttered
Popcorn

Buttered Popcorn

*It's a sinful delight that always
hits the spot! But this luscious
version has no calories.*

Finished Size

Approximately 46" x 64"

Materials

Lion Brand Jiffy chunky-weight mohair-look yarn (3 oz., 135-yd. ball): 14 Goldenrod #187
Size N crochet hook or size to obtain gauge

Gauge

2 dc = 1"
5 rows = 4"

Pattern Stitch

Popcorn: Work 5 dc in next st, drop last lp from hook, insert hook from front to back through top of first st of grp, pick up dropped lp and pull through, ch 1 to complete popcorn.

Directions

Afghan: **Row 1** (RS): Ch 93, dc in 4th ch from hook and in ea rem ch across, turn = 91 dc across.

Row 2: Ch 3 (for first dc), dc in ea dc across, turn.

Row 3: Ch 3 (for first dc), dc in ea of next 4 dc, * popcorn in next dc, dc in ea of next 3 dc, rep from * across, end with dc in ea of last 5 sts = 21 popcorn sts across, turn.

Row 4: Ch 3 (for first dc), dc in ea of next 4 dc, dc in popcorn, * ch 1, sk 1 dc, dc in next dc, ch 1, sk 1 dc, dc in next popcorn, rep from * across, end with dc in ea of last 5 sts, turn.

Row 5: Ch 3 (for first dc), dc in ea of next 4 dc, popcorn in next dc, (ch 1, dc in next dc) across to last 6 sts, ch 1, popcorn in next dc, dc in ea of last 5 sts, turn.

Row 6: Ch 3 (for first dc), dc in ea of next 4 dc, dc in popcorn, (ch 1, dc in next dc) across to last 6 sts, ch 1, dc in popcorn, dc in ea of last 5 sts, turn.

Rows 7–18: Rep Rows 5 and 6 alternately.

Row 19: Ch 3 (for first dc), dc in ea of next 4 dc, popcorn in next dc, (ch 1, dc in next dc) 11 times, ch 1, (popcorn in next dc, dc in next ch-1 sp, dc in next dc, dc in next ch-1 sp) 8 times, popcorn in next dc, (ch 1, dc in next dc) 11 times, ch 1, popcorn in next dc, dc in ea of last 5 sts, turn.

Row 20: Ch 3 (for first dc), dc in ea of next 4 dc, dc in popcorn, (ch 1, dc in next dc) 11 times, ch 1, (dc in popcorn, dc in ea of next 3 dc) 8 times, dc in popcorn, (ch 1, dc in next dc) 11 times, ch 1, dc in popcorn, dc in ea of last 5 sts, turn.

Row 21: Ch 3 (for first dc), dc in ea of next 4 dc, popcorn in next dc, (ch 1, dc in next dc) 11 times, ch 1, popcorn in next dc, dc in ea of next 31 dc, popcorn in next dc, (ch 1, dc in next dc) 11 times, ch 1, popcorn in next dc, dc in ea of last 5 sts, turn.

Row 22: Ch 3 (for first dc), dc in ea of next 4 dc, dc in popcorn, (ch 1, dc in next dc) 11 times, ch 1, dc in popcorn, dc in ea of next 31 dc, dc in popcorn, (ch 1, dc in next dc) 11 times, ch 1, dc in popcorn, dc in ea of last 5 sts, turn.

Row 23: Ch 3 (for first dc), dc in ea of next 4 dc, popcorn in next dc, (ch 1, dc in next dc) 11 times, ch 1, popcorn in next dc, dc in ea of next 7 dc, (popcorn in next dc, dc in ea of next 3 dc) 4 times, popcorn in next dc, dc in ea of next 7 dc, popcorn in next dc, (ch 1, dc in next dc) 11 times, ch 1, popcorn in next dc, dc in ea of last 5 sts, turn.

Row 24: Ch 3 (for first dc), dc in ea of next 4 dc, dc in popcorn, (ch 1, dc in next dc) 11 times, ch 1, dc in popcorn, dc in ea of next 7 dc, dc in popcorn, (ch 1, sk 1 dc, dc in next dc, ch 1, sk 1 dc, dc in popcorn) 4 times, dc in ea of next 7 dc, dc in popcorn, (ch 1, dc in next dc) 11 times, ch 1, dc in popcorn, dc in ea of last 5 sts, turn.

Row 25: Ch 3 (for first dc), dc in ea of next 4 dc, popcorn in next dc, (ch 1, dc in next dc) 11 times, ch 1, popcorn in next dc, dc in ea of next 7 dc, popcorn in next dc, (ch 1, dc in next dc) 7 times, ch 1, popcorn in next dc, dc in ea of next 7 dc, popcorn in next dc, (ch 1, dc in next dc) 11 times, ch 1, popcorn in next dc, dc in ea of last 5 sts, turn.

Row 26: Ch 3 (for first dc), dc in ea of next 4 dc, dc in popcorn, (ch 1, dc in next dc) 11 times, ch 1, dc in popcorn, dc in ea of next 7 dc, dc in popcorn, (ch 1, dc in next dc) 7 times, ch 1, dc in popcorn, dc in ea of next 7 dc, dc in popcorn, (ch 1, dc in next dc) 11 times, ch 1, dc in popcorn, dc in ea of last 5 sts, turn.

Rows 27–56: Rep Rows 25 and 26 alternately.

Row 57: Ch 3 (for first dc), dc in ea of next 4 dc, popcorn in next dc, (ch 1, dc in next dc) 11 times, ch 1, popcorn in next dc, dc in ea of next 7 dc, (popcorn in next dc, dc in ch-1 sp, dc in next dc, dc in ch-1 sp) 4 times, popcorn in next dc, dc in ea of next 7 dc, popcorn in next dc, (ch 1, dc in next dc) 11 times, ch 1, popcorn in next dc, dc in ea of last 5 sts, turn.

Row 58: Ch 3 (for first dc), dc in ea of next 4 dc, dc in popcorn, (ch 1, dc in next dc) 11 times, ch 1, dc in popcorn, dc in ea of next 7 dc, (dc in popcorn, dc in ea of next 3 dc) 4 times, dc in popcorn, dc in ea of next 7 dc, dc in popcorn, (ch 1, dc in next dc) 11 times, ch 1, dc in popcorn, dc in ea of last 5 dc, turn.

Rows 59 and 60: Rep Rows 21 and 22.

Row 61: Ch 3 (for first dc), dc in ea of next 4 dc, popcorn in next dc, (ch 1, dc in next dc) 11 times, ch 1, (popcorn in next dc, dc in ea of next 3 dc) 8 times, popcorn in next dc, (ch 1, dc in next dc) 11 times, ch 1, popcorn in next dc, dc in ea of last 5 sts, turn.

Row 62: Ch 3 (for first dc), dc in ea of next 4 dc, dc in popcorn, (ch 1, dc in next dc) 11 times, ch 1, (dc in popcorn, ch 1, sk 1 dc, dc in next dc, ch 1) 8 times, dc in popcorn, (ch 1, dc in next dc) 11 times, ch 1, dc in popcorn, dc in ea of last 5 sts, turn.

Rows 63–76: Rep Rows 5 and 6 alternately.

Row 77: Ch 3 (for first dc), dc in ea of next 4 dc, (popcorn in next dc, dc in ch-1 sp, dc in next dc, dc in ch-1 sp) across to last 6 sts, popcorn in next dc, dc in ea of last 5 sts, turn.

Row 78: Ch 3 (for first dc), dc in ea of next 4 dc, (dc in popcorn, dc in ea of next 3 dc) across to last 6 sts, dc in popcorn, dc in ea of last 5 sts, turn.

Row 79: Ch 3 (for first dc), dc in ea dc across. Fasten off.

Border: With RS facing and afghan turned to work across top edge, join 2 strands of yarn in corner, ch 3 (for first dc), 4 dc in same st, * popcorn in next st, (dc in ea of next 3 sts, popcorn in next st) across to next corner, 5 dc in corner, (popcorn in first row, 3 dc in next row) across to next corner, 5 dc in corner, rep from * once more, sl st in top of beg ch-3. Fasten off.

Fringe: For each tassel, referring to page 141 of General Directions, cut 6 (10") lengths of yarn. Knot 1 tassel in every other stitch across each short end of afghan.

C

Can I Buy a Vowel?

Can I Buy a Vowel?

Choose letters from our graphed alphabet to stitch any message you please.

Finished Size

Approximately 47" x 51"

Materials

Lion Brand Jiffy chunky-weight mohair-look yarn (3 oz., 135-yd. ball): 10 White #100 (A), 3 Black #153 (B), 3 Red #112 (C)

Size J crochet hook or size to obtain gauge

Gauge

3 sc and 3½ rows = 1"

Block = 7" x 9"

Directions

Note: To change colors, work last yo of last st in prev color with new color, dropping prev color to WS of work. Do not carry yarn not in use across the row.

Plain Block (make 23): With A, ch 22.

Row 1 (RS): Sc in 2nd ch from hook and in ea rem ch across, turn = 21 sc across.

Rows 2–32: Ch 1, sc in ea st across, turn. Fasten off after last row.

Letter Block (make 12): With A, ch 22.

Row 1 (RS): Sc in 2nd ch from hook and in ea rem ch across, turn = 21 sc across.

Row 2: Ch 1, sc in ea st across, turn.

Rows 3–32: Ch 1, work in sc, referring to Placement Diagram and alphabet charts (see pages 20 and 21). Use A for background and B for letters. Read chart from right to left on odd-numbered rows (RS) and left to right on even-numbered rows (WS). Fasten off after last row.

continued on page 20

continued from page 19

Block Border: With RS facing, join C with sl st in any corner, * sc evenly across to next corner, 3 sc in corner, rep from * around, sl st in first sc. Fasten off.

Assembly: Referring to Placement Diagram and using C, whipstitch blocks together.

Afghan Border: Rnd 1: Join C with sl st in any corner, * sc evenly across to next corner, 3 sc in corner, rep from * around, sl st in first sc.

Rnd 2: Ch 1, * sc in ea st to center corner st, 3 sc in corner st, rep from * around, sl st in first sc. Fasten off.

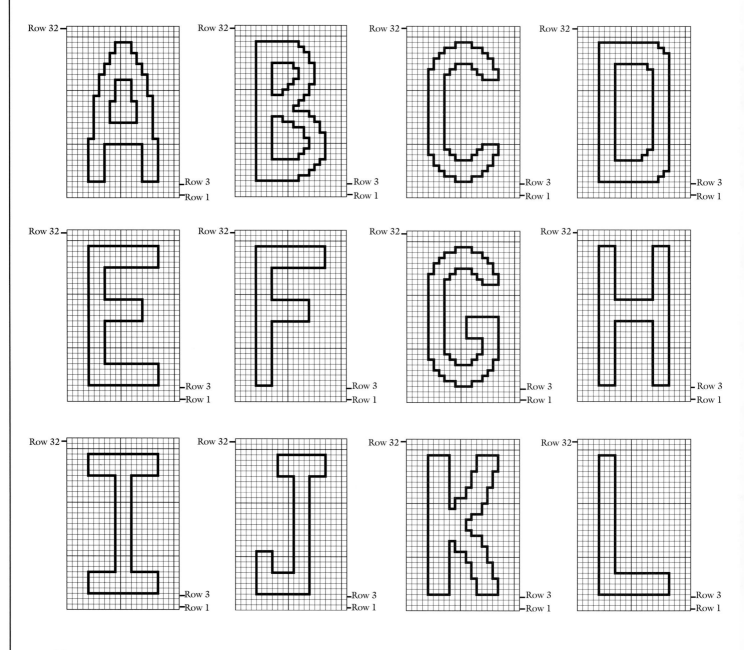

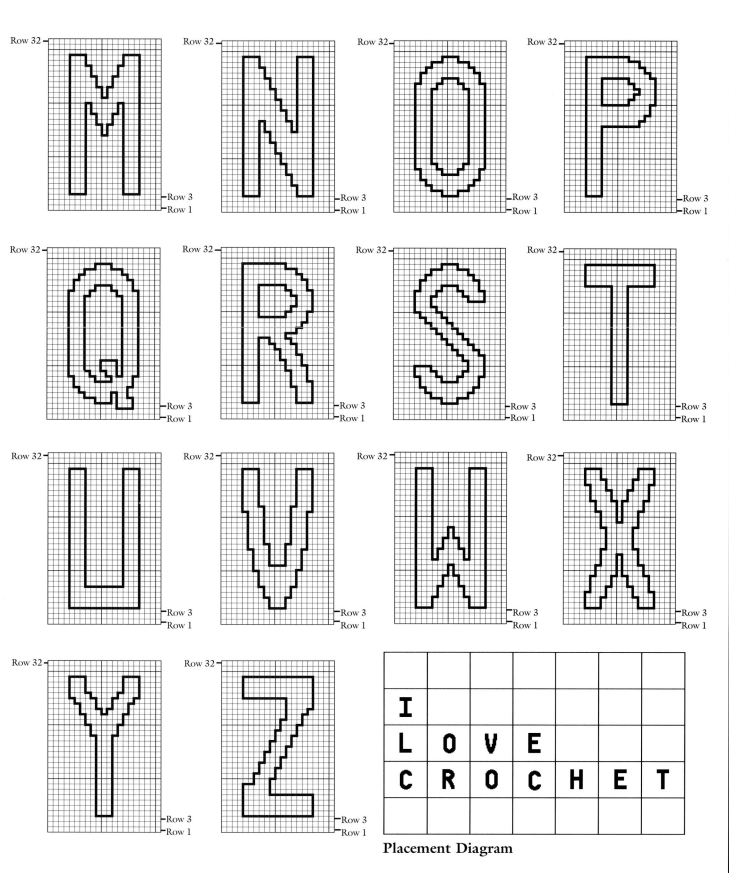

Placement Diagram

Cat's Meow

Cat's Meow

This is dedicated to my two favorite kitties, Ashley and Rhett.

Finished Size

Approximately 45" x 65"

Materials

Lion Brand Jiffy chunky-weight mohair-look yarn (3 oz., 135-yd. ball): 12 Pastel Blue #105 (MC); 2 Lilac #144 (CC); 1 each White #100, Melon #184, Goldenrod #187, Rose #140, Teal #178, Dusty Blue #108, Violet #191

Size J afghan and crochet hooks or size to obtain gauge

Large-eyed tapestry needle

DMC Size 3 Pearl Cotton (16-yd. skein): 2 black

Gauge

7 sts and 6 rows = 2" in afghan st

Square = 20"

Directions

Note: See page 140 for afghan st directions.

Square (make 6): With MC and afghan hook, ch 67, work 60 rows afghan st. Sl st in ea vertical bar across. Fasten off.

Cross-stitch: Referring to photo for colors used for each square, center and cross-stitch 1 cat on each square according to chart and color key, using 1 strand of Jiffy yarn. Backstitch details on each cat using 1 strand of pearl cotton.

Assembly: Afghan is 2 squares wide and 3 squares long. **First Square:** With RS facing and using crochet hook, join CC with sc in bottom right-hand corner of first square. * Ch 5, sk 3 rows along side edge, sc in next row, rep from * to top corner, sc in corner. Fasten off.

2nd Square: With RS facing and using crochet hook, join CC with sc in top left-hand corner of 2nd square. * Ch 2, sl st in center ch of corresponding ch-5 lp on first square, ch 2, sk 3 rows on 2nd square, sc in next row, rep from * across to bottom corner of 2nd square, sc in corner. Fasten off. Cont to join squares as est.

Edging: **Rnd 1:** With RS facing and using crochet hook, join CC with * sc in corner of afghan, ch 5, sc in same corner, [(ch 5, sk 3 sts, sc in next st) across to corner of square, sc in corner of square, ch 5, sc in corner of next square] across to next corner of afghan, rep from * around, sl st in first sc.

Rnd 2: * Ch 5, sc in center ch of next ch-5 lp, rep from * around, sl st in base of beg ch-5.

Rnd 3: Work * 2 sc in next lp, ch 5, sl st in first ch for picot, 2 sc in same lp, rep from * around, sl st in first sc. Fasten off.

Color Key

- ⊙ Cat color (See photo.)
- ☒ White
- ⊙ Bow color (See photo.)

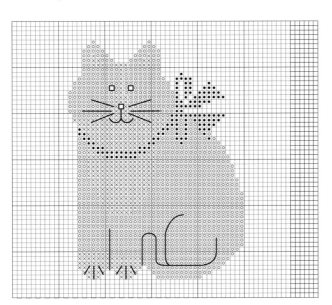

Cross-stitch Chart

D

Daisy
Patchwork

Daisy Patchwork

Whatever the weather, this beauty says,
"Spring is here!"

Finished Size

Approximately 52" x 58"

Materials

Lion Brand Jiffy chunky-weight mohair-look yarn (3 oz., 135-yd. ball): 8 Lilac #144 (MC); 5 each Rose #140 (CC1), White #100 (CC2)

Size N crochet hook or size to obtain gauge

Gauge

Block = 5¾" x 6½"

Directions

Block: Make 40 with Lilac (MC) and Rose (CC1). Make 40 with Lilac (MC) and White (CC2).

With CC, ch 4, join with sl st to form a ring.

Rnd 1: Ch 4 (for first dc and ch-1), (dc in ring, ch 1) 11 times, sl st in 3rd ch of beg ch-4. Fasten off.

Rnd 2: Join MC with sl st in last sl st, ch 2, (yo and pull up a lp in first ch-1 sp, yo and pull through 2 lps on hook) twice, yo and pull through all 3 lps on hook (beg cl made), ch 2, * (yo and pull up a lp in next ch-1 sp, yo and pull through 2 lps on hook) 3 times, yo and pull through all 4 lps on hook (cl made), ch 2, rep from * around, sl st in top of beg cl. Fasten off.

Rnd 3: Join CC with sl st in any ch-2 sp, ch 1, sc in same sp, * yo, working around and over Rnd-2 ch-2, insert hook in Rnd-1 dc below, pull up a long lp, (yo and pull through 2 lps on hook) twice (long dc made), sc in top of next cl, sc in next ch-2 sp, rep from * around, end with long dc in last Rnd-1 dc, sc in last cl, sl st in first sc = 36 sts around.

Rnd 4: Ch 3 (for first dc), dc in same st, * dc in ea of next 7 sts, (2 dc, ch 1, 2 dc) in next st for corner, dc in next st, hdc in next st, sc in ea of next 5 sts, hdc in next st, dc in next st, (2 dc, ch 1, 2 dc) in next st for corner, rep from * once more, sl st in top of beg ch-3. Fasten off.

Rnd 5: Join MC with sl st in any corner sp, ch 1, 2 sc in same sp, * sc in ea st to next corner sp, 3 sc in corner sp, rep from * around, sl st in first sc. Fasten off.

Assembly: Afghan is 8 blocks wide and 10 blocks long. Whipstitch blocks together in checkerboard pattern, making sure all blocks are oriented with dc, hdc, 5 sc, hdc, dc (Rnd 4) edge at top and bottom.

Border: **Rnd 1:** With RS facing, join MC with sl st in any corner, ch 1, * sc in ea st across to next corner, 3 sc in corner, rep from * around, sl st in first sc, turn.

Rnd 2: Ch 1, * sc in ea st to center corner st, 3 sc in corner st, rep from * around, sl st in first sc. Fasten off.

Tassel (make 4): For each tassel, referring to page 141 of General Directions, wrap MC 30 times around a 6" piece of cardboard. At 1 end, slip a 5" yarn length under loops and knot. Cut loops at other end. Loop and tightly wrap a 36" yarn length around tassel 1¼" from top. Secure ends and tuck into tassel. Trim tassel ends even. Stitch 1 tassel to each corner of afghan.

D

Dream-
weaver

Dreamweaver

*Multicolored yarn creates rich shadows
that invite you to lose yourself
in slumber. Sweet dreams!*

Finished Size

Approximately 54" x 78"

Materials

Lion Brand Jiffy chunky-weight mohair-look yarn (2.5 oz., 115-yd. ball): 19 New York multicolor #301
Size I crochet hook or size to obtain gauge

Gauge

Hexagon = 6" diameter

Pattern Stitch

4-DC Popcorn: Work 4 dc in place indicated, drop last lp from hook, insert hook from front to back through top of first st of grp, pick up dropped lp and pull through to complete 4-dc popcorn.

Directions

Hexagon (make 117): Ch 6, join with sl st to form a ring.

Rnd 1: Ch 3 (for first dc), 3 dc in ring, drop last lp from hook, insert hook in top of beg ch-3, pick up dropped lp and pull through (beg popcorn made), (ch 3, 4-dc popcorn in ring) 5 times, ch 3, sl st in top of beg popcorn = 6 popcorns around.

Rnd 2: Sl st into first ch-3 sp, ch 4 (for first tr), 3 tr in same ch-3 sp, (ch 4, 4 tr in next ch-3 sp) 5 times, ch 4, sl st in top of beg ch-4.

Rnd 3: Ch 4 (for first tr), tr in same st, * tr in ea of next 2 tr, 2 tr in next tr, ch 5, sk ch-4 sp, 2 tr in next tr, rep from * around, end with sl st in top of beg ch-4. Fasten off.

Half-Hexagon (make 11): Ch 6, join with sl st to form a ring.

Row 1 (RS): Ch 3 (for first dc), 3 dc in ring, drop last lp from hook, insert hook in top of beg ch-3, pick up dropped lp and pull through (beg popcorn made), (ch 3, 4-dc popcorn in ring) 3 times, turn = 4 popcorns across.

Row 2 (WS): Ch 4 (for first tr), 3 tr in first ch-3 sp, (ch 4, 4 tr in next ch-3 sp) twice, turn.

Row 3: Ch 4 (for first tr), tr in same st, (tr in ea of next 2 tr, 2 tr in next tr, ch 5, sk ch-4 sp, 2 tr in next tr) twice, tr in ea of next 2 tr, 2 tr in last st. Fasten off.

Assembly: With triple stitches aligned, whipstitch hexagons together into 13 rows of 9 hexagons each. In same manner, whipstitch rows together for an afghan 9 hexagons wide and 13 hexagons long. Whipstitch half-hexagons in spaces along side edges of afghan.

Border: **Rnd 1:** With RS facing, join yarn with sl st in any st, sc evenly around afghan, sl st in first sc.

Rnd 2: Sl st in ea sc around. Fasten off.

Terms and Techniques

This afghan makes use of a crochet technique called *multiples*—that is, working more than one stitch into a previous stitch. In several places, for example, you'll be directed to work more than one triple stitch into the same previous stitch.

You'll also be making *popcorn stitches,* a special type of multiple, in which the extra stitches are drawn up to form a raised, dimensional feature in your crocheted fabric. You'll find complete instructions for making the popcorn at the beginning of the directions. For another way to use popcorns in a pattern, see the *Buttered Popcorn* afghan on page 15.

Elegant Rose

Every woman loves roses. Why not give this afghan to a dear friend? It's a bouquet that lasts and lasts.

Finished Size

Approximately 60" x 66"

Materials

Lion Brand Jiffy chunky-weight mohair-look yarn (3 oz., 135-yd. ball): 19 White #100 (MC), 10 Forest Green #131 (CC)

Size K crochet hook or size to obtain gauge

Gauge

Square = 6"

Pattern Stitch

SC Decrease (sc dec): Pull up a lp in ea of next 2 sts, yo and pull through all lps on hook (sc dec over 2 sts made).

Directions

Rose Square (make 55): **Rnd 1** (RS): With MC, ch 2, work 9 sc in 2nd ch from hook.

Note: Do not sl st to join at end of rnds. Work in bk lps only in a spiral for Rnds 2 and 3. Use a scrap of contrasting yarn or a small safety pin to mark beg of ea rnd.

Rnd 2 (RS): Work 2 sc in ea st around = 18 sts around.

Rnd 3 (RS): Work * 2 sc in next st, sc in next st, rep from * around, sl st in bk lp of first sc (sl st counts as 1 st), turn = 28 sts around.

Rnd 4 (WS): Ch 1, working in bk lps only (ft lps sk on prev row), (2 dc in next st, dc in next st, 2 dc in next st, sc dec over next 2 sts) 6 times, (2 hdc in next st, hdc in next st, 2 hdc in next st, sc dec over next 2 sts) 4 times, 2 sc in next st, sc in next st, 2 sc in next st, pull up a lp in next st, pull up a lp in next st and pull through both lps on hook, turn.

Rnd 5 (RS): Working through both lps of ea st around, sl st in first sc, (2 sc in next st, sc in next st) twice, 2 sc in next st, [* sl st in next st, (2 hdc in next st, hdc in next st) twice, 2 hdc in next st **] 3 times, [sl st in next st, (2 dc in next st, dc in next st) twice, 2 dc in next st] 6 times, rep from * to ** once, end with sl st in base of tch on prev row. Fasten off.

Rnd 6: With RS facing, join CC in bk lp of any st on Rnd 3, ch 3 (for first dc), dc in same st, * hdc in ea of next 2 sts, sc in ea of next 2 sts, hdc in ea of next 2 sts, 3 dc in next st for corner, rep from * around, ending with 1 dc in beg corner, sl st in top of beg ch-3, turn.

Rnds 7 and 8: Ch 3 (counts as first dc), dc in same st, * dc in ea st to center corner st, 3 dc in corner st, rep from * around, ending with 1 dc in beg corner, sl st in top of beg ch-3, turn. Fasten off after last rnd.

Circle in Square (make 55): **Rnds 1–3:** With CC, work as for Rnds 1–3 of Rose Square.

Rnds 4–6: With MC, work as for Rnds 6–8 of Rose Square. Fasten off after last rnd.

Assembly: Afghan is 10 squares wide and 11 squares long. Whipstitch squares together in a checkerboard pattern.

Border: **Rnd 1:** With RS facing, join MC in any corner, * sc evenly across to next corner, 3 sc in corner, rep from * around, sl st in first sc. Fasten off.

Rnd 2: With RS facing, join CC in any corner, * sc in ea st to center corner st, 3 sc in corner st, rep from * around, sl st in first sc. Fasten off.

Edelweiss

Edelweiss

*A throw of flowers and lace is very feminine
and pretty. And since you make this afghan in
squares, it's a perfect take-along project.*

Finished Size

Approximately 41½" x 53"

Materials

Lion Brand Jamie Pompadour sportweight yarn
(1.75 oz., 196-yd. skein): 11 skeins White #200
Size H crochet hook or size to obtain gauge

Gauge

Square = 5¾"

Directions

Square (make 63): Ch 6, join with sl st to form a
ring.

Rnd 1: Ch 1, 16 sc in ring, sl st in first sc = 16
sts.

Rnd 2: Ch 6 (for first dc and ch 3), sk 2 sts, (dc
in next st, ch 3, sk 1 st) 7 times, sl st in 3rd ch of
beg ch-6 = 8 ch-3 sps around.

Rnd 3: Ch 1, work petal of (sc, hdc, 5 dc, hdc,
sc) in ea ch-3 sp around, sl st in first sc = 8 petals
around.

Rnd 4: (Sc bet next 2 sc, ch 6) 8 times, sl st in
first sc = 8 ch-6 lps around.

Rnd 5: Ch 1, (sc, hdc, 6 dc, hdc, sc) in ea ch-6
lp around, sl st in first sc = 8 petals around.

Rnd 6: Sl st in 2nd dc of next Rnd-5 petal, ch 1,
sc in same st as ch-1, ch 6, sk 2 dc, sc in next dc,
(ch 6, sc in 2nd dc of next petal, ch 6, sk 2 dc, sc in
next dc) 7 times, ch 3, dc in first sc = 16 lps
around.

Rnd 7: Ch 3 (for first dc), 3 dc in last lp of prev
rnd, * ch 4, sc in next lp, (ch 6, sc in next lp) twice,
ch 4 **, (4 dc, ch 4, 4 dc) in next lp, rep from * 3
times more, ending last rep at **, (4 dc, ch 4) in
same lp as beg, sl st in top of beg ch-3. Fasten off.

Assembly: Afghan is 7 squares wide and 9 squares
long. Join yarn with sl st in corner sp of first
square, ch 3, sl st in corresponding corner sp on
2nd square, * ch 3, sl st in next ch-lp on first
square, ch 3, sl st in corresponding ch-lp on 2nd
square, rep from * to next corner sp on first
square, ch 3, sl st in corresponding corner sp on
next square. Cont as est until all squares have been
joined. Fasten off.

Border: **Rnd 1:** With WS facing, join yarn with sl
st in top right corner of afghan, work 198 sc evenly
spaced across to next corner, 259 sc evenly spaced
across to next corner, 198 sc evenly spaced across
to next corner, 258 sc evenly spaced across to beg
corner.

Rnd 2: Ch 1, sc in first st, * sk 2 sts, 5 dc in next
st, sk 2 sts, sc in next st, rep from * around, end
with sl st in first sc. Fasten off.

F

Football
Fever

Football Fever

For weekends on the couch watching the big game, what a perfect afghan to give the man who loves football!

Finished Size

Approximately 42" x 56"

Materials

Lion Brand Keepsake Sayelle* worsted-weight yarn (6 oz., 312-yd. skein): 2 each Cocoa Brown #123 (A), White #100 (B); 5 Evergreen #130 (C); 1 Black #153 (D)

Size J crochet hook or size to obtain gauge

Gauge

3 sc and 3½ rows = 1"

Directions

Note: To change colors, work last yo of last st in prev color with new color, dropping prev color to WS of work. Do not carry yarn not in use across the row.

Afghan: With A, ch 121.

Row 1 (RS): Sc in 2nd ch from hook and in ea rem ch across, turn = 120 sc across.

Rows 2–95: Ch 1, work in sc, changing colors according to chart (see page 34). Read chart from right to left on odd-numbered rows (RS) and left to right on even-numbered rows (WS).

Rows 96–190: Reverse chart and cont as est, working from Row 95 back to Row 1. Fasten off all yarns after Row 190.

Border: **Rnd 1:** With RS facing, join B with sl st in any corner, * sc in ea st to next corner, 3 sc in corner, rep from * around, sl st in first sc.

Rnds 2–4: Ch 1, * sc in ea st to center corner st, 3 sc in corner st, rep from * around, sl st in first sc. Fasten off after last rnd.

continued on page 34

continued from page 33

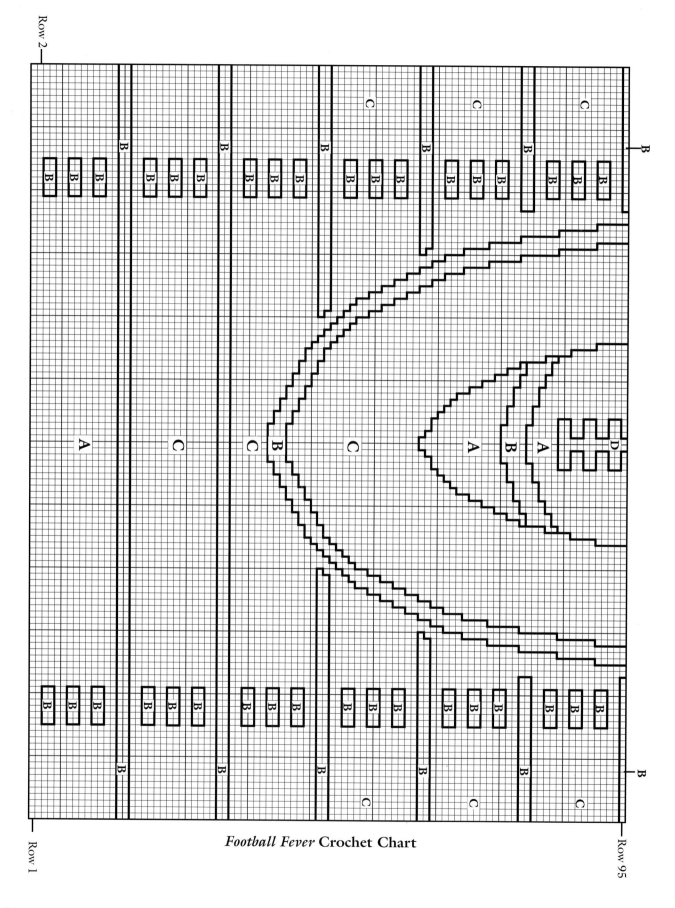

Football Fever Crochet Chart

Row 2

Row 1

Row 95

F

*Fish in
the Sea*

Fish in the Sea

*This afghan reminds me of an aquarium
I once had. It was such a joy for me
to watch the fish swim.*

Finished Size

Approximately 40" x 53"

Materials

Lion Brand Jiffy chunky-weight mohair-look yarn: 10 (2.5 oz., 115-yd. balls) Newport multicolor #320 (MC); 2 (3 oz., 135-yd. balls) Goldenrod #187 (A); 1 (3 oz., 135-yd. ball) each Black #153 (B), Scarlet #113 (C), White #100 (D); 3 (3 oz., 135-yd. balls) Teal #178 (E)

Size J crochet hook or size to obtain gauge

Gauge

3 sc and 3½ rows = 1"

Directions

Note: To change colors, work last yo of last st in prev color with new color, dropping prev color to WS of work. Do not carry yarn not in use across the row.

Center Panel: With MC, ch 91.

Row 1 (RS): Sc in 2nd ch from hook and in ea rem ch across, turn = 90 sts across.

Rows 2–18: Ch 1, sc in ea st across, turn.

Rows 19–170: Referring to Fish Crochet Chart, work in sc, changing colors according to chart. Read chart from right to left on odd-numbered rows (RS) and left to right on even-numbered rows (WS). Fasten off all yarns after Row 170.

Border: With RS facing, join MC with sl st in corner of center panel, sc evenly across ea side edge of center panel. Fasten off.

Row 1: With RS facing, join E with sl st in top left corner of center panel, * work 3 sc in corner, 126 sc evenly spaced across to next corner, 3 sc in corner, 88 sc evenly spaced across to next corner, rep from * once more, turn.

Rows 2–18: Referring to Wave Crochet Chart, work in sc, changing colors according to chart. Turn work at end of each row. For top and bottom short edges of afghan, work pat rep of 30 sts (shown on chart) 3 times. For long side edges of afghan, work pat rep of 30 sts (shown on chart) 4 times. Read chart from right to left on odd-numbered rows (RS) and left to right on even-numbered rows (WS). Fasten off all yarns after Row 18.

Finishing: Use matching yarn to whip-stitch border edges together.

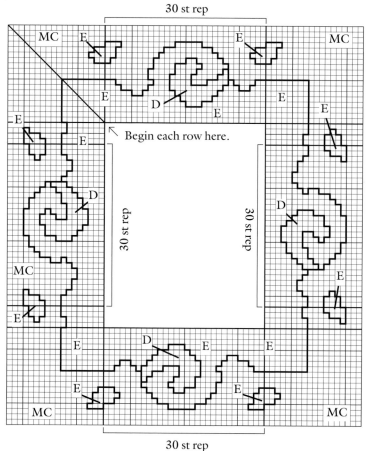

Wave Crochet Chart

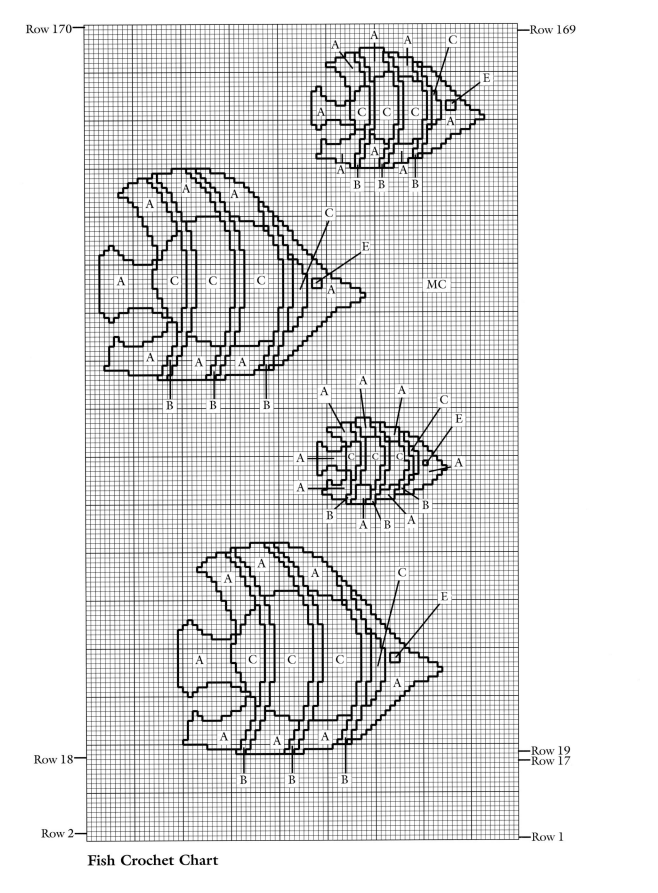

Fish Crochet Chart

Giggles and Squiggles

Giggles and Squiggles

Tiptoe in for a peek at Nicholas napping. This baby blanket worked from easy-to-read charts makes a cozy coverlet.

Finished Size

Approximately 40" x 46"

Materials

Lion Brand Jamie Pompadour sportweight yarn: 10 (1.5 oz., 170-yd. skeins) Playtime print #243 (MC); 2 (1.75 oz., 196-yd. skeins) each Pastel Green #269 (A), Pastel Blue #206 (B), Pink #201 (C), Lavender #244 (D)

Size G crochet hook or size to obtain gauge

Gauge

9 sc = 2"

Directions

Note: To change colors, work last yo of last st in prev color with new color, dropping prev color to WS of work. Do not carry yarn not in use across the row.

Ovals Block (make 1): **Row 1** (RS): With MC, ch 87, sc in 2nd ch from hook and in ea rem ch across, turn = 86 sc across.

Row 2: Ch 1, sc in ea sc across, turn.

Rows 3–30: Ch 1, work in sc, changing colors according to Ovals Crochet Chart. Read chart from right to left on odd-numbered rows (RS) and left to right on even-numbered rows (WS).

Rep Rows 3–30, 3 times more = 4 pat rep.

Last Row: With MC, sc in ea st across. Fasten off all yarns.

Border: With RS facing, join MC with sl st in any corner of block, * sc evenly across to next corner of block, 2 sc in corner, rep from * around, sl st in first sc. Fasten off.

Arches Block (make 1): Work as for Ovals Block, referring to Arches Crochet Chart for color changes. Fasten off all yarns after last row.

Border: Work border around block as for Ovals Block.

Bars Block (make 1): **Rows 1 and 2:** Rep Rows 1 and 2 as for Ovals Block.

Rows 3–30: Work in sc according to Bars Crochet Chart (see page 40).

Rows 31–108: Cont in sc, working colors as est in Row 30.

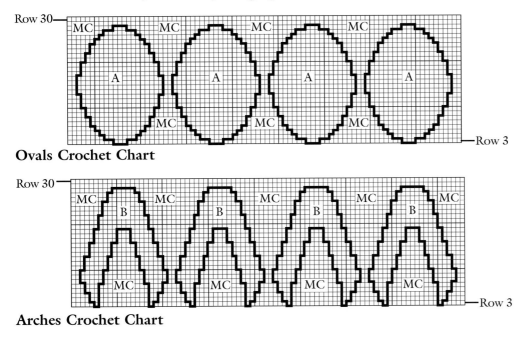

Row 30

Row 3

Ovals Crochet Chart

Row 30

Row 3

Arches Crochet Chart

continued on page 40

continued from page 39

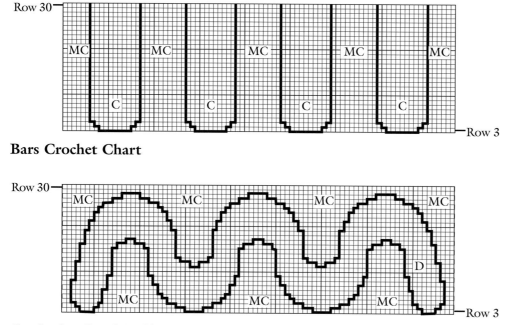

Bars Crochet Chart

Squiggles Crochet Chart

Row 109: Rep Row 4 of chart.
Row 110: Rep Row 3 of chart.
Rows 111 and 112: With MC, sc in ea st across, turn. Fasten off all yarns after Row 112.

Border: Work border around block as for Ovals Block.

Squiggles Block (make 1): Work as for Ovals Block, referring to Squiggles Crochet Chart for color changes. Fasten off all yarns after last row.

Border: Work border around block as for Ovals Block.

Assembly: Afghan is 2 blocks square. Referring to photo, whipstitch blocks together.

Border: **Rnd 1:** With RS facing, join MC with sl st in any corner, * sc in ea st to next corner, 3 sc in corner, rep from * around, sl st in first sc.
Rnds 2–5: Ch 1, * sc in ea st to center corner st, 3 sc in corner st, rep from * around, sl st in first sc. Fasten off after last rnd.

G

Granny's Delight

Granny's Delight

My grandmother would have loved this; it's like a pattern she once made.

Finished Size

Approximately 48" x 68"

Materials

Lion Brand Keepsake Sayelle* worsted-weight yarn (6 oz., 312-yd. skein): 6 Cream #098 (MC), 2 Light Mauve #140 (A), 2 Queen's Blue #108 (B), 3 Burgundy #142 (C)

Size I crochet hook or size to obtain gauge

Gauge

Large square = 5"

Pattern Stitch

Cluster (cl): (Yo, insert hook where indicated and pull up a lp, yo and pull through 2 lps on hook) 3 times, yo and pull through rem 4 lps on hook to complete cl.

Directions

Large Square (make 96): With A, ch 4, join with sl st to form a ring.

Rnd 1 (RS): Ch 3 (for first dc), 2 dc in ring, ch 3, (3 dc in ring, ch 3) 3 times, sl st in top of beg

ch-3 = 4 ch-3 sps and 12 dc around. Fasten off.

Rnd 2: With RS facing, join B with sl st in any ch-3 sp, ch 3 (for first dc), (2 dc, ch 3, 3 dc) in same sp, ch 1, * (3 dc, ch 3, 3 dc) in next ch-3 sp, ch 1, rep from * around, sl st in top of beg ch-3. Fasten off.

Rnd 3: With RS facing, join C with sl st in any ch-3 sp, ch 3 (for first dc), (2 dc, ch 3, 3 dc) in same sp, ch 1, * 3 dc in next ch-1 sp, ch 1, (3 dc, ch 3, 3 dc) in corner ch-3 sp, ch 1, rep from * around, end with sl st in top of beg ch-3. Fasten off.

Rnd 4: With RS facing, join MC with sc in any ch-3 sp, ch 2, sc in same sp, ch 3, * (sc in next ch-1 sp, ch 3) twice, (sc, ch 2, sc) in corner ch-3 sp, rep from * around, end with sl st in first sc, turn.

Rnd 5 (WS): Ch 1, * (sc, ch 1, sc) in first ch-3 sp, cl in bk lp only of next sc, [(sc, ch 1, sc) in next ch-3 sp, cl in bk lp only of next sc] twice, (sc, ch 3, sc) in corner ch-2 sp, cl in bk lp only of next sc, rep from * around, end with sl st in first sc. Fasten off.

Corner Square (make 4): With B, ch 4, join with sl st to form a ring.

Rnd 1: Rep Rnd 1 as for Large Square. Fasten off.

Rnd 2: With C, rep Rnd 2 as for Large Square. Fasten off.

Rnd 3: With RS facing, join MC with sc in any ch-3 sp, ch 2, sc in same sp, ch 3, * sc in next ch-1 sp, ch 3, (sc, ch 2, sc) in next corner ch-3 sp, ch 3, rep from * twice more, sl st in first sc, turn.

Rnd 4 (WS): Ch 1, * [(sc, ch 1, sc) in ch-3 sp, cl in bk lp only of next sc] twice, (sc, ch 3, sc) in corner ch-2 sp, rep from * around, end with sl st in first sc. Fasten off.

Long Border Strip (make 2): **Foundation** (WS): With A, (ch 3, cl in 2nd ch from hook) 56 times, ch 2 = 56 cl total. Fasten off.

Rnd 1: With RS facing, join B with sl st in ch bet first 2 cl, ch 3 (for first dc), 2 dc in same ch, ch 1, working in ch bet cl, (3 dc in next ch, ch 1) across to last ch bet cl, [3 dc, (ch 3, 3 dc) twice] in ch at top of last cl, ch 1, working in free lps of ea ch bet cl, (3 dc in next ch, ch 1) across to last ch, [3 dc, (ch 3, 3 dc) twice] in ch at bottom of first cl, ch 1, sl st in top of beg ch-3. Fasten off.

Rnd 2: With RS facing and holding Strip vertically, join C with sl st in top right corner ch-3 sp, ch 3 (for first dc), (2 dc, ch 3, 3 dc) in same corner sp, ch 1, (3 dc, ch 3, 3 dc) in next corner sp, ch 1, (3 dc in next ch-1 sp, ch 1) across to next corner ch-3 sp, [(3 dc, ch 3, 3 dc) in corner sp, ch 1] twice, (3 dc in next ch-1 sp, ch 1) across, sl st in top of beg ch-3. Fasten off.

Rnd 3: With RS facing and holding Strip vertically, join MC with sc in top right corner ch-3 sp, ch 2, sc in same sp, * ch 3, sc in next ch-1 sp, ch 3, (sc, ch 2, sc) in next corner ch-3 sp, ch 3, (sc in next ch-1 sp, ch 3) across to next corner ch-3 sp **, (sc, ch 2, sc) in corner sp, rep from * to ** once more, sl st in first sc, turn.

Rnd 4 (WS): Ch 1, * [(sc, ch 1, sc) in next ch-3 sp, cl in bk lp only of next sc] across to next corner ch-2 sp, (sc, ch 3, sc) in corner sp, cl in bk lp only of next sc, rep from * around, end with sl st in first sc. Fasten off.

Short Border Strip (make 2): **Foundation** (WS): With A, (ch 3, cl in 2nd ch from hook) 36 times, ch 2 = 36 cl total. Fasten off.

Rnd 1: With B, work as for Rnd 1 of Long Border Strip.

Rnd 2: With C, work as for Rnd 2 of Long Border Strip.

Rnds 3 and 4: With MC, work as for Rnds 3 and 4 of Long Border Strip.

Assembly: Whipstitch Large Squares together to make a panel 8 squares wide and 12 squares long. Whipstitch 1 Short Border Strip to each end of center panel. Whipstitch 1 Corner Square to each end of each Long Border Strip. Whipstitch 1 strip to each side edge of afghan.

Edging: **Rnd 1:** With RS facing, join MC with sc in any corner sp, ch 2, sc in same sp, * ch 1, (sc in next cl, ch 1, sc in next ch-1 sp, ch 1) across to next corner, (sc, ch 2, sc) in corner sp, rep from * around, end with sl st in first sc.

Rnd 2: * (Ch 1, sl st) twice in corner sp, (ch 1, sl st in next ch-1 sp) across to next corner ch-2 sp, rep from * around, end with sl st in first st. Fasten off.

Terms and Techniques

Although this afghan is made with basic stitches, beginners who make it will learn lots of useful crochet techniques, including *clusters,* working in the round, and quick-stitch strips.

Here's a special hint about *clusters:* these involve holding many loops on the hook until you yarn over and work them all off. Use your index finger to hold the loop closest to the hook in place. This will keep all the loops from slipping off before you are finished.

H

Hudson's Bay Memory

Hudson's Bay Memory

This is ideal for rustic decorating.

Finished Size

Approximately 40" x 58"

Materials

Lion Brand Jiffy chunky-weight mohair-look yarn (3 oz., 135-yd. ball): 7 Fisherman #99 (A); 2 each Black #153 (B), Goldenrod #187 (C), Red #112 (D), Evergreen #130 (E)

Size J crochet hook or size to obtain gauge

Gauge

3 sc and 3½ rows = 1"

Directions

Afghan: With A, ch 121.

Row 1: Sc in 2nd ch from hook and in ea rem ch across, turn = 120 sc across.

Row 2: Ch 1, sc in ea sc across, turn.

Rep Row 2, working colors in foll sequence: 6 more rows A, 12 rows B, 6 rows A, 12 rows C, 6 rows A, 12 rows D, 6 rows A, 12 rows E.

To make points (small bars): Work * 2 rows A. Next row: Work 105 sc with A, 12 sc with B, 3 sc with A, turn. Next row: Work 3 sc with A, 12 sc with B, 105 sc with A, turn. Rep from * 3 times more. Cont working in sc with A until this stripe measures 18" from last E stripe.

Rep Row 2, working colors in foll sequence: 12 rows E, 6 rows A, 12 rows D, 6 rows A, 12 rows C, 6 rows A, 12 rows B, 8 rows A. Fasten off.

Border: **Rnd 1:** Using matching colors, join yarn with sl st in corner, * sc evenly to next corner, 3 sc in corner, rep from * around, leaving a long tail of each color to work next rnd.

Rnd 2: Using long tails of yarn from prev rnd, work around afghan in crab st (reverse sc) from left to right (instead of right to left). Fasten off.

H
Hooked
on
Checkers

Hooked on Checkers

Of course I love games! When I was a child, my favorite was checkers. Now, with this big checkerboard, I can play again.

Finished Sizes

Checkerboard: Approximately 39" x 42"
Checker: Approximately 3" diameter

Materials

Lion Brand Keepsake Sayelle* worsted-weight yarn (6 oz., 312-yd. skein): 2 each Scarlet #113 (A), Black #153 (B); 1 Cream #098 (C)
Size J crochet hook or size to obtain gauge

Gauge

Square = 4½"
Checker = 3" diameter

Directions

Square (make 32 ea with A and B): **Row 1:** Ch 13, sc in 2nd ch from hook and in ea rem ch across, turn = 12 sc across.

Rows 2–14: Ch 1, sc in ea sc across, turn. Fasten off after last row.

Side Edge Border: With square turned to work across 1 side edge, join matching yarn with sl st in corner, work 11 sc evenly spaced across to next corner. Fasten off. Rep to work 11 sc across rem side edge.

Square Border: Join C with sl st in any corner, * sc evenly across to next corner, 3 sc in corner, rep from * around, sl st in first sc. Fasten off.

Panel Assembly: Arrange 32 squares in checkerboard pattern to form a panel 8 squares wide and 4 rows long. Whipstitch squares together. In same manner, whipstitch remaining squares together to form 2nd panel.

Panel Border: With RS facing, join C with sl st in any corner, * sc evenly across to next corner, 3 sc in corner, rep from * around, sl st in first sc. Fasten off. Whipstitch panels together.

Checkerboard Border: **Rnd 1:** With RS facing, join C with sl st in any corner, * sc evenly across to next corner, 3 sc in corner, rep from * around, sl st in first sc.

Rnd 2: * Sc in ea st to center corner st, 3 sc in corner st, rep from * around, sl st in first sc. Fasten off.

Circle (make 24 ea with A and B): Ch 4, join with sl st to form a ring.

Rnd 1: Ch 2 (for first hdc), 12 hdc in ring, sl st in top of beg ch-2 = 13 hdc around.

Rnd 2: Ch 2 (for first hdc), hdc in same st, 2 hdc in ea st around, sl st in top of beg ch-2 = 26 hdc around. Fasten off.

Checker Assembly: With wrong sides facing, holding 2 circles together, and working through back loops only, join matching yarn with sc in any st, working through both layers, sc in ea st around, sl st in first sc. Fasten off.

I

Ice Crystals

Ice Crystals

Just right to warm you up in icy weather, this pretty afghan is made with easy-stitch scallops and picots.

Finished Size

Approximately 42" x 62"

Materials

Lion Brand Jiffy chunky-weight mohair-look yarn (3 oz., 135-yd. ball): 13 White #100

Sizes I and K crochet hooks or size to obtain gauge

Gauge

2 pat rep = 7" with size K hook

Directions

Afghan: With size K hook, ch 146 to measure 45".

Row 1 (WS): Sc in 2nd ch from hook, * ch 5, sk 3 ch, sc in next ch, rep from * across, turn = 36 ch-5 lps across.

Row 2 (RS): Ch 5, * sc in center ch of next ch-5 lp, 8 dc in next lp, sc in center ch of next lp, ch 5, rep from * across, end with ch 2, dc in last sc, turn.

Row 3: Ch 1, sc in last dc of prev row, * dc in first dc of next 8-dc grp, (ch 3, sl st in 3rd ch from hook for picot, dc in next dc of same grp) 7 times (shell made), sc in center of next lp, rep from * across, end with sc in 3rd ch of tch, turn.

Row 4: Ch 8, * sc in 3rd picot of shell, ch 5, sk 1 picot, sc in next picot of same shell, ch 5, dc in next sc bet shells, ch 5, rep from * across, end with ch 5, dc in last sc, turn.

Rep Rows 2–4 for pat until piece measures about 62" from beg, ending after last rep of Row 3, turn. Do not fasten off.

Border: With RS facing, afghan turned to work down left side edge, and using size I hook, (sc evenly across to next corner, 3 sc in corner) twice, sc evenly across to next corner. Do not work border across top edge of afghan. Fasten off.

Terms and Techniques

Working scallops: Make a chain loop or space and, on the next row, work several stitches into it. The multiple stitches spread out to make a fan or scallop effect. For a similar pattern, see the afghan *Jewels of the Nile* on page 56.

Making picots: After a double crochet, chain three, then slip stitch in the third chain from the hook (the chain right at the top of the double crochet). This makes a little bump called a picot.

*I Wish
I Could
Fly*

I Wish I Could Fly

*Nicholas's nursery is decorated with airplanes.
Maybe one day he'll love flying planes
as much as his father does.*

Finished Size

Approximately 36" x 43"

Materials

Lion Brand Jamie Pompadour sportweight yarn
(1.75 oz., 196-yd. skein): 10 Pastel Blue #206
(A); 2 White #200 (B); 1 each Pastel Yellow #257
(C), Pastel Green #269 (D), Pink #201 (E)
Size G crochet hook or size to obtain gauge
2 yards ⅞"-wide white satin ribbon
White sewing thread
Stuffing

Gauge

19 sc and 22 rows = 4"

Directions

Note: Work each color area with a
separate ball of yarn. To change
colors, work last
yo of last st in
prev color
with new
color, drop-
ping prev
color to WS
of work. Do
not carry yarn
not in use across the row.

Afghan: **Row 1** (RS): With A, ch
161, sc in 2nd ch from hook and in ea
rem ch across, turn = 160 sc across.
Rows 2–225: Ch 1, sc in ea st
across. Fasten off after last row.

Edging: **Rnd 1:** Join B with sl st
in any corner, * sc evenly across
to next corner, 3 sc in
corner, rep from * around, sl st in first sc.
Rnds 2–4: Ch 1, * sc in ea st to center corner st,
3 sc in corner st, rep from * around, sl st in first sc.
Rnd 5: * Sl st in ea of next 2 sc, (sc, ch 3, sc) in
next sc, rep from * around, sl st in same st as first sl
st. Fasten off.

Airplane: Beg at tail of airplane, with D, ch 53.
Row 1: Sc in 2nd ch from hook and in ea rem
ch across.

Rows 2–113: Ch 1, work in sc,
changing colors and shaping airplane, according to chart. Read
chart from right to left on odd-
numbered rows (RS) and left to
right on even-numbered rows (WS).
Note: Cross-stitch mouth with E
after airplane is complete.

To shape airplane: To inc 1 st,
work 2 sc in 1 st. To
dec 1 st, pull up
a lp in ea of
next 2 sts, yo
and pull
through all 3
lps on hook.
To inc 2 or
more sts at beg of
row, ch 1 more than the required
number of sts to be added, sc in 2nd
ch from hook and in ea rem ch; at end
of row, attach a separate strand of yarn
and ch required number of sts to be
added, then complete row by working
1 sc in ea ch of added ch. To dec 2 or
more sts, at beg of row, sl st across
required number of sts; at end of
row, leave required number of sts
unworked.

Row 113

Row 2 — — Row 1

Airplane Crochet Chart

continued on page 52

continued from page 51

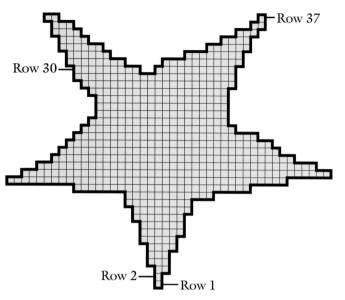

Row 37
Row 30
Row 30
Row 2
Row 1

Star Crochet Chart

Star (make 3): With C, ch 2.

Row 1: Sc in 2nd ch from hook, turn.

Rows 2–37: Ch 1, work in sc, shaping star according to chart. Read chart from right to left on odd-numbered rows (RS) and left to right on even-numbered rows (WS).

To shape star: Refer to directions for shaping airplane (see page 51). On Row 30, ch 1, sc in ea of next 9 sts, sk 2 sts, attach a separate ball of yarn, ch 1, sc in ea of next 11 sts. Fasten off after last row of chart.

Finishing: Referring to photo, position airplane and stars on front of afghan. Cut ribbon lengths for contrails and stitch to afghan. Stitch airplane and stars to afghan, stuffing lightly before closing.

52

J

*Jigsaw
Fun*

Jigsaw Fun

When I was younger, my mother and I would sit up half the night putting jigsaw puzzles together. I still love them!

Finished Size

Approximately 42½" x 57"

Materials

Lion Brand Jamie 4 Kids worsted-weight yarn (2 oz., 140-yd. skein): 5 each Buttercup #157 (A), Flag Blue #109 (B); 4 Fire Engine Red #113 (C); 3 Evergreen #130 (D)

Size J crochet hook or size to obtain gauge

Gauge

6 sc and 7 rows = 2"

Directions

Note: To change colors, work last yo of last st in prev color with new color, dropping prev color to WS of work. Do not carry yarn not in use across the row.

Afghan: With A, ch 40, attach B and ch 40, attach another ball of A and ch 41 = 121 ch.

Row 1 (RS): With A, sc in 2nd ch from hook and in ea of next 39 ch, sc in ea of next 40 ch with B, sc in ea of last 40 ch with A, turn = 120 sc across.

Rows 2–200: Ch 1, work in sc, changing colors according to chart. Read chart from right to left on odd-numbered rows (RS) and left to right on even-numbered rows (WS). Fasten off after last row.

Border: With RS facing and matching color to edge, join yarn with sl st in corner, sc evenly across each side edge of afghan.

Rnd 1: With RS facing, join B in any corner, * sc in ea st across to next corner, 3 sc in corner, rep from * around, sl st in first sc.

Rnds 2–5: Ch 1, * sc in ea st to center corner st, 3 sc in corner st, rep from * around, sl st in first sc. Fasten off after last rnd.

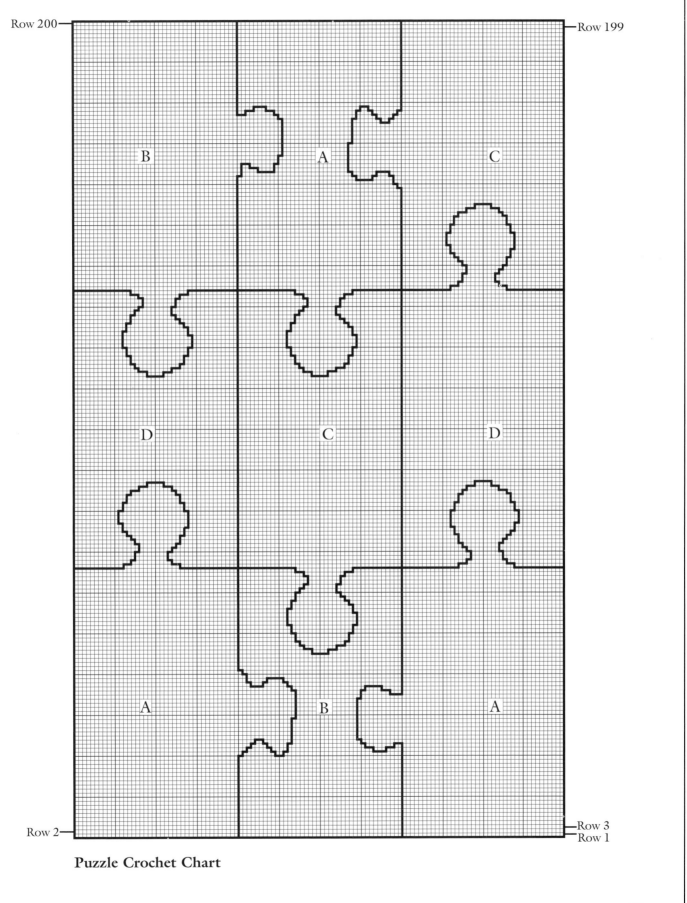

B   A   C

D   C   D

A   B   A

Puzzle Crochet Chart

J
Jewels
of the
Nile

Jewels of the Nile

*I've always been fascinated by the River Nile.
Stitch this up in exotic colors and you can
have an adventure in crochet.*

Finished Size

Approximately 51" x 72"

Materials

Lion Brand Jiffy chunky-weight mohair-look yarn (3 oz., 135-yd. ball): 4 each Teal #178 (A), Violet #191 (B), Mulberry #190 (C), Black #153 (D)

Size J crochet hook or size to obtain gauge

Gauge

1 fan pat rep and 4 pat rows = 3"

Directions

Note: To change colors, work last yo of last st in prev color with new color.

Afghan: With A, ch 172 very loosely.

Row 1 (RS): Sc in 2nd ch from hook, * ch 1, sk 4 ch, (tr, ch 2) 4 times in next ch, tr in same ch (fan made), ch 1, sk 4 ch, sc in next ch, rep from * across, change to B in last st, turn = 17 fans across. Fasten off A.

Row 2: With B, ch 5, * sk (sc, ch-1, and 1 tr), dc in next ch-2 sp, ch 3, sk (1 tr and next ch-2 sp), sc in next tr, ch 3, sk (next ch-2 sp and 1 tr), dc in next ch-2 sp **, ch 2, rep from * across, ending last rep at **, ch 1, tr in last sc, turn.

Row 3: Ch 6, (tr, ch 2, tr) in first ch-1 sp, * ch 1, sk (next dc and ch-3), sc in next sc, ch 1, sk (next ch-3 and 1 dc) **, (tr, ch 2) 4 times in next ch-2 sp, tr in same sp (fan made), rep from * across, ending last rep at **, (tr, ch 2) twice in ch-5 sp at end of row, tr in same sp, change to C in last st, turn. Fasten off B.

Row 4: With C, ch 1, sc in first tr, * ch 3, sk (next ch-2 sp and 1 tr), dc in next ch-2 sp, ch 2, sk (next tr, ch-1, sc, and ch-1), dc in next ch-2 sp, ch 3, sk (next tr and ch-2 sp), sc in next tr, rep from * across, end with sc in 4th ch of tch, turn.

Row 5: Ch 1, sc in first sc, * ch 1, sk (ch-3 and dc), (tr, ch 2) 4 times in next ch-2 sp, tr in same sp (fan made), ch 1, sk (next dc and ch-3), sc in next sc, rep from * across, change to D in last st, turn. Fasten off C.

Row 6: With D, rep Row 2.

Row 7: With D, rep Row 3, change to A in last st. Fasten off D.

Row 8: With A, rep Row 4.

Row 9: With A, rep Row 5, change to B in last st. Fasten off A.

Rows 10–96: Rep Rows 2–9 for pat.

Row 97: With A, ch 1, sc in first tr, * 2 sc in next ch-3 sp, sc in next dc, sc in next ch-2 sp, sc in next dc, 2 sc in next ch-3 sp, sc in next sc, rep from * across. Fasten off.

Border: **Rnd 1:** With WS facing, join C with sl st in any corner, * sc evenly across to next corner, 3 sc in corner, rep from * around, sl st in first sc. Fasten off.

Rnd 2: With WS facing, join B with sl st in center st of any corner, ch 1, working in crab st (reverse sc), from left to right (instead of right to left), sc in ea st around, sl st in first sc. Fasten off.

K

*Kiss
Me
Quick*

Kiss Me Quick

*Rosy lips on a field of blue are sure
to make you smile.*

Finished Size

Approximately 46" x 65"

Materials

Lion Brand Jiffy Chunky bulky-weight yarn (3 oz., 120-yd. ball): 12 Blue #109 (MC), 5 Red #112 (A)

Size K crochet hook or size to obtain gauge

Gauge

3 pat rep = 7"

11 pat rows = 8"

Directions

Note: To change colors, work last yo of last st in prev color with new color, dropping prev color to WS of work. Divide red yarn into separate small balls and work each red area with 1 small ball; do not carry red yarn across the row. Carry blue yarn loosely across the row.

Afghan: With MC, ch 122 very loosely.

Row 1 (RS): Sc in 2nd ch from hook, * sk 2 ch, 5 dc in next ch (shell made), sk 2 ch, sc in next ch, rep from * across, turn = 20 shells across.

Row 2: Ch 3 (for first dc), 2 dc in first sc, * sk 2 dc of next shell, sc in center dc of same shell, sk last 2 dc of shell, 5 dc in next sc, rep from * across, end with 3 dc in last sc, turn.

Row 3: Ch 1, sc in first dc, * sk 2 dc, 5 dc in next sc, sk 2 dc of next shell, sc in next dc, rep from * across, end with sc in top of tch and change to A, turn.

Row 4: With A, ch 3 (for first dc), 2 dc in first sc, * change to MC and (sk 2 dc, sc in next dc, sk 2 dc, 5 dc in next sc) 3 times, sk 2 dc, sc in next dc, change to B and sk 2 dc, 5 dc in next sc, rep from * across, end with 3 dc in last sc with A, turn.

Row 5: With A, ch 1, sc in first dc, * sk 2 dc, 5 dc in next sc, change to MC and (sk 2 dc, sc in next dc, sk 2 dc, 5 dc in next sc) twice, sk 2 dc, sc in next dc, change to A and sk 2 dc, 5 dc in next sc, sk 2 dc, sc in next dc, rep from * across, end with sc in top of tch with A, turn.

Row 6: With A, ch 3 (for first dc), 2 dc in first sc, sk 2 dc, sc in next dc, sk 2 dc, 5 dc in next sc, * change to MC and sk 2 dc, sc in next dc, sk 2 dc, 5 dc in next sc, sk 2 dc, sc in next dc, change to A and (sk 2 dc, 5 dc in next sc, sk 2 dc, sc in next dc) twice, sk 2 dc, 5 dc in next sc, rep from * across, end with 3 dc in last sc with A, turn.

Row 7: Rep Row 5. Fasten off each ball of A.

Rows 8–11: With MC, rep Rows 2 and 3 alternately.

Row 12: With MC, ch 3 (for first dc), 2 dc in first sc, * sk 2 dc, sc in next dc, sk 2 dc, 5 dc in next sc, sk 2 dc, sc in next dc, change to A and sk 2 dc, 5 dc in next sc, change to MC and (sk 2 dc, sc in next dc, sk 2 dc, 5 dc in next sc) twice, rep from * across, end with 3 dc in last sc with MC, turn.

Row 13: With MC, ch 1, sc in first dc, * sk 2 dc, 5 dc in next sc, sk 2 dc, sc in next dc, change to A and sk 2 dc, 5 dc in next sc, sk 2 dc, sc in next dc, sk 2 dc, 5 dc in next sc, change to MC and sk 2 dc, sc in next dc, sk 2 dc, 5 dc in next sc, sk 2 dc, sc in next dc, rep from * across, end with sc in top of tch with MC, turn.

Row 14: With MC, ch 3 (for first dc), 2 dc in first sc, * sk 2 dc, sc in next dc, change to A and (sk 2 dc, 5 dc in next sc, sk 2 dc, sc in next dc) twice, sk 2 dc, 5 dc in next sc, change to MC and sk 2 dc, sc in next dc, sk 2 dc, 5 dc in next sc, rep from * across, end with 3 dc in last sc with MC, turn.

Row 15: Rep Row 13. Fasten off each ball of A.

Rows 16–19: With MC, rep Rows 2 and 3 alternately.

Rows 20–90: Rep Rows 4–19 for pat. Do not fasten off MC after last row.

Border: With RS facing and MC, * sc evenly across to corner, 3 sc in corner, rep from * around, sl st in first sc. Fasten off.

K

King of
the
Jungle

King of the Jungle

This afghan is a dramatic accent for your home. It also makes a great gift for animal-lovers or those born under the sign of Leo.

Finished Size

Approximately 42" x 56"

Materials

Lion Brand Jiffy chunky-weight mohair-look yarn (3 oz., 135-yd. ball): 9 Taupe #125, 4 Black #153

Size J afghan and crochet hooks or size to obtain gauge

Large-eyed tapestry needle

Gauge

6 sts and 5 rows = 2" in afghan st

Directions

Note: See page 140 for afghan st directions.

Afghan: With Black and afghan hook, ch 130, work 6 rows afghan st.

Next row: Pull up 8 lps with Black, join Taupe and pull up 114 lps, join another ball of Black and pull up 8 lps.

Work Row 1, Step 2 of afghan st, using colors as est.

Work 142 more rows afghan st, using colors as est. Fasten off Taupe.

With Black, work 6 more rows afghan st. Sl st in ea vertical bar across. Fasten off.

Border: **Rnd 1:** With RS facing and using crochet hook, join Black with sl st in corner, * sc in ea st across to next corner, 3 sc in corner, rep from * around, sl st in first sc.

Rnd 2: Ch 1, working in crab st (reverse sc), from left to right (instead of right to left), sc in ea st around, sl st in first sc. Fasten off.

Cross-stitch: Using 1 strand of Black yarn, cross-stitch lion on Taupe panel of afghan according to chart. Using 1 strand of Black yarn, outline-stitch whiskers and eyes and make French knots on muzzle as indicated on chart.

Key   -------   Outline Stitch   •   French Knot

Cross-stitch Chart

L

Lovely Poppies

Lovely Poppies

Step into the garden and pick this striking pattern for your next afghan.

Finished Size

Approximately 53" x 70"

Materials

Lion Brand Jiffy chunky-weight mohair-look yarn (3 oz., 135-yd. ball): 17 Fisherman #99 (MC); 10 Scarlet #113 (A); 2 each Evergreen #130 (B), Black #153 (C), Goldenrod #187 (D)

Size I crochet hook or size to obtain gauge

Gauge

Rows 1–5 (triangle) = 4" x 4" x 5½"
Square = 8½"

Pattern Stitches

Beginning Block (Beg Block): Ch 5, turn, 3 dc in 4th ch from hook.

Block: Sl st in ch-3 sp of next Block, ch 3, 3 dc in same sp.

Directions

Note: Square is worked diagonally from corner to corner.

To change colors, work last yo of last st in prev color with new color, dropping prev color to WS of work. Do not carry yarn not in use across the row.

Square (make 48): **Row 1** (RS): With MC, ch 5, 3 dc in 5th ch from hook, turn = 1 Block.

Row 2 (WS): With MC, work Beg Block, sl st around beg ch of prev Block (see Diagram A on page 64), ch 3, 3 dc in same sp (see Diagram B on page 64), turn = 2 Blocks.

Row 3: With MC, work Beg Block, sl st in ch-3 sp of first Block, ch 3, 3 dc in same sp, work Block, turn = 3 Blocks.

Row 4: With MC, work Beg Block, sl st in ch-3

continued on page 64

continued from page 63

sp of first Block, ch 3, 3 dc in same sp, work 2 Blocks, turn = 4 Blocks.

Row 5: With MC, work Beg Block, sl st in ch-3 sp of first Block, ch 3, 3 dc in same sp, work 1 Block with D, work 2 Blocks with MC, turn = 5 Blocks.

Row 6: With MC, work Beg Block, sl st in ch-3 sp of first Block, ch 3, 3 dc in same sp, work 2 Blocks with D, work 2 Blocks with MC = 6 Blocks.

Row 7: With MC, work Beg Block, sl st in ch-3 sp of first Block, ch 3, 3 dc in same sp, work 1 Block with A, work 1 Block with D, work 1 Block with A, work 2 Blocks with MC = 7 Blocks.

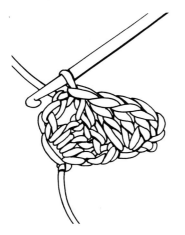

Diagram A

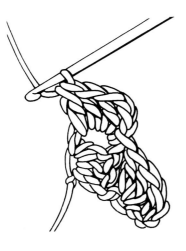

Diagram B

Row 8: With MC, work Beg Block, sl st in ch-3 sp of first Block, ch 3, 3 dc in same sp, work 4 Blocks with A, work 2 Blocks with MC = 8 Blocks.

Row 9: With MC, work Beg Block, sl st in ch-3 sp of first Block, ch 3, 3 dc in same sp, work 2 Blocks with A, work 1 Block with MC, work 2 Blocks with MC = 9 Blocks.

Row 10: With MC, work Beg Block, sl st in ch-3 sp of first Block, ch 3, 3 dc in same sp, (work 2 blocks with A, work 2 Blocks with MC) twice = 10 Blocks.

Row 11: With MC, work Beg Block, sl st in ch-3 sp of first Block, ch 3, 3 dc in same sp, work 2 Blocks with A, work 3 Blocks with MC, work 2 Blocks with A, work 2 Blocks with MC = 11 Blocks.

Row 12: With MC, work Beg Block, sl st in ch-3 sp of first Block, ch 3, 3 dc in same sp, work 2 Blocks with A, work 4 Blocks with MC, work 2 Blocks with A, work 2 Blocks with MC = 12 Blocks.

Row 13 (beg dec): With MC, sl st in ea of first 3 dc and in first ch-3 sp, ch 3, 3 dc in same sp, work 2 Blocks with A, work 2 Blocks with MC, work 1 Block with D, work 2 Blocks with MC, work 2 Blocks with A, work 1 Block with MC, sl st in ch-3 sp of last Block, turn = 11 Blocks.

Row 14: With MC, sl st in ea of first 3 dc, sl st in first ch-3 sp with A, (ch 3, 3 dc in same sp) with A, work 1 Block with A, work 1 Block with MC, work 4 Blocks with C, work 1 Block with MC, work 2 Blocks with A, sl st in ch-3 sp of last Block, turn = 10 Blocks.

Row 15: With A, sl st in ea of first 3 dc and in first ch-3 sp, ch 3, 3 dc in same sp, work 2 Blocks with A, work 3 Blocks with C, work 3 Blocks with A, sl st in ch-3 sp of last Block, turn = 9 Blocks.

Row 16: With A, sl st in ea of first 3 dc, sl st in first ch-3 sp with MC, ch 3, 3 dc in same sp with MC, work 2 Blocks with A, work 2 Blocks with C, work 2 Blocks with A, work 1 Block with MC, sl st in ch-3 sp of last Block, turn = 8 Blocks.

Row 17: With MC, sl st in ea of first 3 dc and in first ch-3 sp, ch 3, 3 dc in same sp, work 2 Blocks with A, work 1 Block with C, work 2 Blocks with A, work 1 Block with MC, sl st in ch-3 sp of last Block, turn = 7 Blocks.

Row 18: With MC, sl st in ea of first 3 dc and in

first ch-3 sp, ch 3, 3 dc in same sp, work 4 Blocks with A, work 1 Block with MC, sl st in ch-3 sp of last Block, turn = 6 Blocks.

Row 19: With MC, sl st in ea of first 3 dc and in first ch-3 sp, ch 3, 3 dc in same sp, work 3 Blocks with B, work 1 Block with MC, sl st in ch-3 sp of last Block, turn = 5 Blocks.

Row 20: With MC, sl st in ea of first 3 dc and in first ch-3 sp, ch 3, 3 dc in same sp, work 2 Blocks with B, work 1 Block with MC, sl st in ch-3 sp of last Block, turn = 4 Blocks.

Row 21: With MC, sl st in ea of first 3 dc and in first ch-3 sp, ch 3, 3 dc in same sp, work 1 Block with B, work 1 Block with MC, sl st in ch-3 sp of last Block, turn = 3 Blocks.

Row 22: With MC, sl st in ea of first 3 dc and in first ch-3 sp, ch 3, 3 dc in same sp, work 1 Block with MC, sl st in ch-3 sp of last Block, turn = 2 Blocks.

Row 23: With MC, sl st in ea of first 3 dc, sl st in first ch-3 sp with B, ch 3, 3 dc in same sp, sl st in ch-3 sp of last Block. Fasten off.

Assembly: Referring to Assembly Diagram, join 4 squares to form each large block. With right sides facing and working through both loops, whipstitch squares together. Repeat to join remaining squares to form 11 more large blocks. Whipstitch blocks together in 4 rows of 3 blocks each.

Border: With RS facing, join MC with sl st in same ch as any corner Block, * ch 2, 3 dc in same st, (sk next Block, sl st in same ch as next Block, ch 2, 3 dc in same st) across to next corner, sl st in base of first dc on corner Block, ch 2, 3 dc in same st **, sl st in same ch as corner Block, rep from * 3 times more, ending last rep at **, sl st in first sl st. Fasten off.

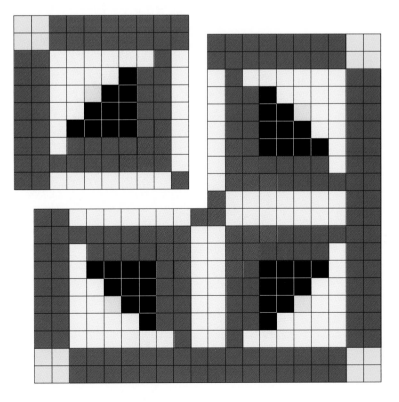

Assembly Diagram

L

Little Lambs

Little Lambs

Lambs are such gentle creatures.
Make these with an easy loop stitch that
gives them soft, pettable coats.

Finished Size

Approximately 47" x 57"

Materials

Lion Brand Jiffy chunky-weight mohair-look yarn (3 oz., 135-yd. ball): 10 Dusty Grey #151 (MC), 3 Black #153 (A), 4 Oatmeal #123 (B)

Size J crochet hook or size to obtain gauge

Gauge

3 sc and 3½ rows = 1"

Pattern Stitch

Loop stitch (lp st): (See page 141.) On WS, work 1 lp st in ea sc as foll (referring to chart): insert hook in next st, lp yarn over index finger of left hand from front to back to form a 1" lp, pick up yarn under finger (keeping lp on finger to RS of work) and draw through st, yo and pull through both lps on hook to complete sc st (1 lp st made).

Directions

Note: To change colors, work last yo of last st in prev color with new color, dropping prev color to WS of work. Do not carry yarn not in use across the row.

Plain Square (make 10): With MC, ch 31.

Row 1: Sc in 2nd ch from hook and in ea rem ch across, turn = 30 sc across.

Rows 2–34: Ch 1, sc in ea sc across, turn. Fasten off after last row.

Lamb Square A (make 5): With MC, ch 31.

Row 1: Sc in 2nd ch from hook and in ea rem ch across, turn = 30 sc across.

Rows 2–34: Work in sc and lp st according to chart for Lamb A, changing colors as indicated. Read chart from right to left on odd-numbered rows (RS) and left to right on even-numbered rows (WS). Fasten off after last row.

Lamb Square B (make 5): Work as for Lamb Square A, referring to Lamb B chart.

Assembly: Whipstitch squares together as desired.

Border: **Rnd 1:** Join MC with sl st in corner, * sc evenly across to next corner, 3 sc in corner, rep from * around, sl st in first sc. Fasten off.

Rnds 2–5: Join A with sl st in corner st, * sc in ea st to center corner st, 3 sc in corner st, rep from * around, sl st in first sc. Fasten off A after Rnd 5.

Rnds 6–13: Join B with sl st in corner, rep Rnd 2. Fasten off B after Rnd 13.

Rnds 14–17: Join A with sl st in corner, rep Rnd 2. Fasten off after last rnd.

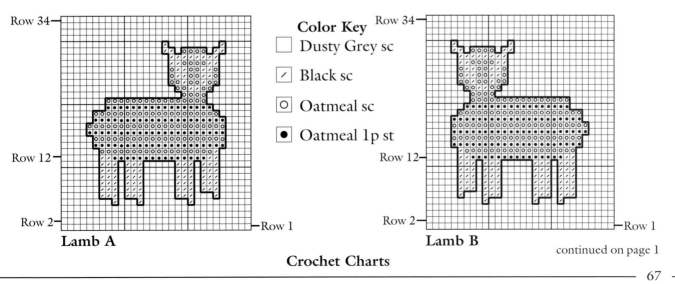

Color Key

☐ Dusty Grey sc

⟋ Black sc

⊙ Oatmeal sc

● Oatmeal lp st

Lamb A

Lamb B

Crochet Charts

continued on page 1

Mix and Match

Mix and Match

This versatile pattern makes gift-giving a snap. Stitch easy panels in your friend's favorite colors and join.

Finished Size

Approximately 45" x 57"

Materials

Lion Brand Jiffy chunky-weight mohair-look yarn: 7 (2.5 oz., 115-yd. balls) Madison multicolor #326 (MC); 4 (3 oz., 135-yd. balls) each Sienna #143 (A), Iris #145 (B); 3 (3 oz., 135-yd. balls) Oatmeal #123 (C)

Size J crochet hook or size to obtain gauge

Gauge

3 sts = 1"
1 pat rep (Rows 2–7) = 2½"
Panel = 14" wide

Directions

Left Panel (make 1): With A, ch 43.

Row 1 (RS): Dc in 4th ch from hook and in ea rem ch across, turn = 41 dc across.

Row 2: Ch 1, sc in ea st across, turn.

Row 3: Ch 1, sc in first st, insert hook in next st, yo and pull up a lp, ch 3 in this lp only for bead, yo and pull through 2 lps on hook (bead st made), push bead to RS of work, sc in next st, (bead st in next st, sc in next st) across, turn = 20 bead sts across.

Row 4: Ch 1, sc in ea st across, turn.

Rows 5 and 6: Rep Rows 3 and 4.

Row 7: Ch 3 (for first dc), dc in ea st across, turn.

Rows 8–43: Rep Rows 2–7, 6 times. Fasten off after Row 43.

Rows 44–79: With MC, rep Rows 2–7, 6 times. Fasten off after Row 79.

Rows 80–115: With B, rep Rows 2–7, 6 times. Fasten off after Row 115.

Rows 116–151: With MC, rep Rows 2–7, 6 times. Fasten off after last row.

Center Panel (make 1): With B, ch 43.

Row 1: Dc in 4th ch from hook and in ea rem ch across, turn.

Rows 2–37: Rep Rows 2–7 as for Left Panel, 6 times. Fasten off after Row 37.

Rows 38–73: With C, rep Rows 2–7 as for Left Panel, 6 times. Fasten off after Row 73.

Rows 74–109: With MC, rep Rows 2–7 as for Left Panel, 6 times. Fasten off after Row 109.

Rows 110–151: With B, rep Rows 2–7 as for Left Panel, 7 times. Fasten off after last row.

Right Panel (make 1): With MC, ch 43.

Row 1: Dc in 4th ch from hook and in ea rem ch across, turn.

Rows 2–43: Rep Rows 2–7 as for Left Panel, 7 times. Fasten off after Row 43.

Rows 44–79: With A, rep Rows 2–7 as for Left Panel, 6 times. Fasten off after Row 79.

Rows 80–115: With C, rep Rows 2–7 as for Left Panel, 6 times. Fasten off after Row 115.

Rows 116–151: With A, rep Rows 2–7 as for Left Panel, 6 times. Fasten off after last row.

Assembly: Whipstitch panels together.

Border: Matching yarn color to edge of afghan, join yarn with sl st in corner, sc evenly across ea side edge to next corner. Fasten off.

Rnd 1: Join MC with sl st in any corner, ch 3 (for first dc), * dc in ea st across to next corner, (dc, ch 2, dc) in corner, rep from * around, sl st in top of beg ch-3.

Rnd 2: Ch 3 (for first dc), * dc in ea st across to next corner, (dc, ch 2, dc) in corner sp, rep from * around, sl st in top of beg ch-3. Fasten off.

Merry Christmas Wreaths

Merry Christmas Wreaths

Christmas is my favorite holiday. It's a time of special family memories.

Finished Size

Approximately 53" x 79"

Materials

Lion Brand Keepsake Sayelle* worsted-weight yarn (6 oz., 312-yd. skein): 9 Cream #098 (MC), 5 Evergreen #130 (A), 2 Scarlet #113 (B)

Size J crochet hook or size to obtain gauge

Gauge

Octagon = 6½"

Pattern Stitch

Cluster (cl): (Yo, insert hook where indicated and pull up a lp, yo and pull through 2 lps on hook) 3 times, yo and pull through all 4 lps on hook = cl made.

Directions

Octagon (make 96): **Rnd 1** (RS): With MC, ch 4, 11 dc in 4th ch from hook, sl st in top of beg ch-4 = 12 dc around.

Rnd 2: Ch 3 (for first dc), dc in same st, 2 dc in ea dc around, sl st in top of beg ch-3 = 24 dc around. Fasten off.

Rnd 3: With WS facing, join A with sc in any st, cl in bk lp only of next st, sc in both lps of same st, * sc in next dc, cl in bk lp only of next dc, sc in both lps of same dc, rep from * around, sl st in first sc, turn = 12 cl and 24 sc around.

Rnd 4 (RS): Ch 1 (for first sc), sc in first sc, ch 1, sk next st, * sc in next st, ch 1, sk next st, rep from * around, sl st in first sc, turn = 18 ch-1 sps around.

continued on page 72

continued from page 71

Rnd 5 (WS): Ch 1 (for first sc), sc in first ch-1 sp, cl in bk lp only of next sc, sc in next ch-1 sp, cl in bk lp only of next sc, 2 sc in next ch-1 sp, cl in bk lp only of next sc, * (sc in next ch-1 sp, cl in bk lp only of next sc) twice, 2 sc in next ch-1 sp, cl in bk lp only of next sc, rep from * around, sl st in first sc = 18 cl and 24 sc around. Fasten off.

Rnd 6: With RS facing, join MC with sl st in any st, ch 3 (for first dc), dc in same st and in ea of next 6 sts, * 2 dc in next st, dc in ea of next 6 sts, rep from * around, sl st in top of beg ch-3 = 48 dc around.

Rnd 7: Ch 4 (for first dc and ch 1), sk next dc, dc in next dc, ch 1, sk next dc, (dc, ch 3, dc) in next dc, ch 1, sk next dc, * (dc in next dc, ch 1, sk next dc) twice, (dc, ch 3, dc) in next dc, ch 1, sk next dc, rep from * around, sl st in 3rd ch of beg ch-4 = 8 ch-3 sps around. Fasten off.

Bow: With B, leaving a 10"-long tail of yarn at beg, ch 4, (dc, ch 2, sl st) in 4th ch from hook = center made, ch 3, (dc, ch 2, sl st) in center, (ch 4, sl st in 2nd ch from hook and in ea of next 2 ch, sl st in center) twice, make a 10"-long ch for ribbon. Fasten off.

Referring to photo, place bow on wreath. Thread needle with yarn tail and stitch bow to wreath by wrapping yarn tail around center. With same yarn, secure ends of bow streamers to wreath. Weave ribbon chain through wreath and tack in place.

Square (make 77): **Rnd 1** (RS): With MC, ch 5, (dc, ch 1) 11 times in 5th ch from hook, sl st in 4th ch of beg ch-5, turn = 12 ch-1 sps around.

Rnd 2 (WS): Ch 1, sc in first ch-1 sp, cl in bk lp only of next dc, sc in next ch-1 sp, * ch 1, sc in next ch-1 sp, cl in bk lp only of next dc, sc in next ch-1 sp, rep from * around, ch 1, sl st in first sc, turn = 6 cl around.

Rnd 3 (RS): Ch 1, sc in first ch-1 sp, * ch 1, sk next sc, sc in next cl, ch 1, sk next sc, (dc, ch 3, dc) in next ch-1 sp, ch 1, sk next sc, sc in next cl, ch 1, sk next sc, sc in next ch-1 sp, ch 1, sk next sc, (dc, ch 3, dc) in next cl, ch 1, sk next sc **, sc in next ch-1 sp, rep from * to ** once more, sl st in first sc. Fasten off.

Assembly: With all wreaths right side up and using MC, whipstitch 2 octagons together from center ch of 1 corner ch-3 sp to center ch of next corner ch-3 sp. Repeat to join pieces into 8 strips of 12 octagons each. Whipstitch squares to inside corners of 7 strips (see Assembly Diagram). Whipstitch strips together.

Triangle: **Row 1:** With RS facing, join MC with sl st at Point A as shown on Diagram, ch 3 (for first dc), dc in ea of next 4 ch-sps of same octagon, dc in next 5 ch-sps of next octagon, turn = 10 dc across.

Row 2: Ch 3 (for first dc), [(yo, pull up a lp in next dc, yo and pull through 2 lps on hook) twice, yo and pull through all 3 lps on hook] 4 times, dc in last dc. Fasten off, leaving an 8" tail of yarn. Weave yarn tail through ft lp only of ea Row-2 st, pull up tightly, and secure. Rep Rows 1 and 2 in ea sp around afghan.

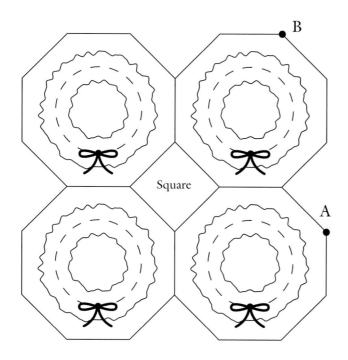

B

Square

A

Assembly Diagram

Edging: **Rnd 1:** With RS facing, join MC with sc in ch-3 sp at Point B as shown on Diagram, place marker around sc just made, (ch 1, sc in next dc) 4 times, * [ch 1, sc in next ch-3 sp, (ch 1, sc) 4 times evenly spaced across ends of rows of Triangle, ch 1, sc in next ch-3 sp, (ch 1, sc in next dc) 4 times] across to next corner **, [ch 1, sc in next ch-3 sp, place marker around sc just made, (ch 1, sc in next dc) 4 times] twice, rep from * 3 times more, ending last rep at **, ch 1, sc in next ch-3 sp, place marker around sc just made, (ch 1, sc in next dc) 4 times, ch 1, sl st in first sc.

Rnd 2: Ch 1 (for first sc), sc in first ch-1 sp, (ch 1, sc in next ch-1 sp) across to marked st, * ch 2, sc in next ch-1 sp, (ch 1, sc in next ch-1 sp) across to next marked st, rep from * around, ch 2, sl st in first sc.

Rnd 3: Sl st into first ch-1 sp, * (ch 1, sl st in next ch-1 sp) across to next ch-2 sp, (ch 1, sl st) twice in next ch-2 sp, rep from * around, ch 1, sl st in first sl st. Fasten off.

Nursery Sampler

Nursery Sampler

*Here's a sweet baby blanket with soft,
soothing colors, hearts and stars, and even
a little lesson—A, B, C and 1, 2, 3.*

Finished Size

Approximately 33" x 38"

Materials

Lion Brand Jamie Pompadour sportweight yarn (1.75 oz., 196-yd. skein): 4 Pastel Yellow #257 (A), 3 White #200 (B), 1 Pink #201 (C), 3 Lavender #244 (D), 1 Pastel Blue #206 (E)

Size G crochet hook or size to obtain gauge

Gauge

19 sc and 22 rows = 4"

Directions

Note: To change colors, work last yo of last st in prev color with new color, dropping prev color to WS of work. Do not carry yarn not in use across the row.

Center Panel (make 1): With A, ch 34.

Row 1: Sc in 2nd ch from hook and in ea rem ch across, turn = 33 sc across.

Row 2: Ch 1, sc in ea sc across, turn.

Rep Row 2 until piece measures approximately 11½" from beg.

Border: Row 1: Ch 1, * sc in ea st across edge to next corner, 3 sc in corner, rep from * around. Fasten off.

Row 2: Join B in center st of any corner, ch 1, work 3 sc in corner st, drop B, * join C and sc in ea st to center corner st, join B and work 3 sc in corner st, rep from * twice more, join C and sc in ea st across to beg corner, turn. Do not join.

Rows 3–11: Ch 1, sc in ea C st with C, sc in ea B st with B, working 3 sc with B in ea center corner st, turn. Fasten off after Row 11.

Rows 12–22: Join D in center st of any corner, * sc in ea st to center corner st, 3 sc in corner st, rep from * around, turn. Fasten off after last row.

End Panels A and B (make 1 ea): **Row 1** (RS): With B, ch 72, sc in 2nd ch from hook and in ea rem ch across, turn = 71 sc across.

Row 2: Ch 1, sc in ea sc across, turn.

Rows 3–28: Ch 1, work in sc, changing colors according to Chart A or B. Read chart from right to left on odd-numbered rows (RS) and left to right on even-numbered rows (WS). Fasten off after last row.

Side Panels C and D (make 1 ea): **Row 1** (RS): With B, ch 25, sc in 2nd ch from hook and in ea rem ch across, turn = 24 sc across.

Row 2: Ch 1, sc in ea sc across, turn.

Rows 3–165: Ch 1, work in sc, changing colors according to Chart C or D (see page 76). Read chart from right to left on odd-numbered rows (RS) and left to right on even-numbered rows (WS). Fasten off after last row.

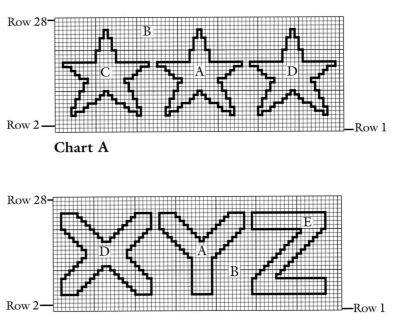

Chart A

Chart B

continued on page 76

continued from page 75

Assembly: Use matching yarn to whipstitch open corner of center panel. Referring to photo, whipstitch end and side panels to center panel.

Border: **Rnd 1:** With RS facing, join A with sl st in any corner, * sc in ea st to next corner, 3 sc in corner, rep from * around, sl st in first sc.

Rnds 2–11: Ch 1, * sc in ea st to center corner st, 3 sc in corner st, rep from * around, sl st in first sc. Fasten off after Rnd 11.

Rnd 12: Join D with sl st in any corner, * sc in ea st to center corner st, 3 sc in corner st, rep from * around, sl st in first sc.

Rnds 13–22: Ch 1, * sc in ea st to center corner st, 3 sc in corner st, rep from * around, sl st in first sc. Fasten off after Rnd 22.

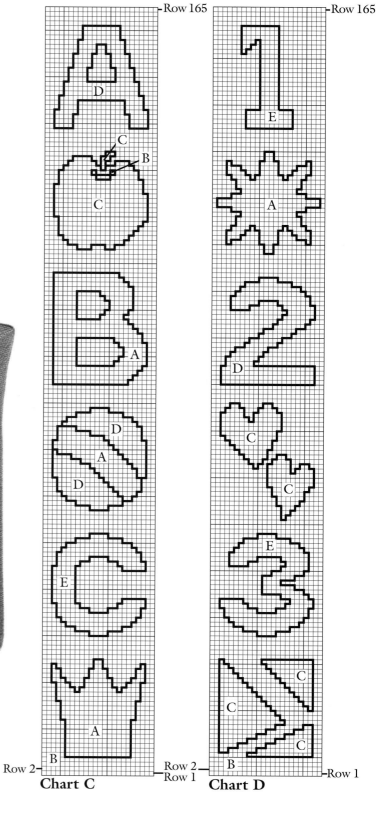

Chart C

Chart D

Night Blooms

Night-blooming cactus grow outside my window. It's nice to see them full of flowers on a starry night.

Finished Size

Approximately 44" x 57"

Materials

Lion Brand Jiffy Chunky bulky-weight yarn (3 oz., 120-yd. ball): 8 Black #153 (A); 7 Pine #132 (B); 1 each Sienna #143 (C), Pastel Yellow #157 (D)

Size J crochet hook or size to obtain gauge

Gauge

6 sc and 7 rows = 2"

Directions

Note: To change colors, work last yo of last st in prev color with new color, dropping prev color to WS of work. Carry yarn not in use loosely across the row.

Afghan: With A, ch 121 loosely.

Row 1 (RS): Referring to chart for color changes, sc in 2nd ch from hook and in ea rem ch across, turn = 120 sc across.

Rows 2 and foll: Ch 1, work in sc, changing colors according to chart. Read chart from right to left on odd-numbered rows (RS) and left to right on even-numbered rows (WS). Rep Rows 1–56, 3 times. Rep Rows 57–66 once. Fasten off all yarns.

Border: Rnd 1: With RS facing, join A with sl st in any corner, * sc evenly across to next corner, 3 sc in corner, rep from * around, sl st in first sc.

Rnds 2–7: Ch 1, * sc in ea st to center corner st, 3 sc in corner st, rep from * around, sl st in first sc. Fasten off after last rnd.

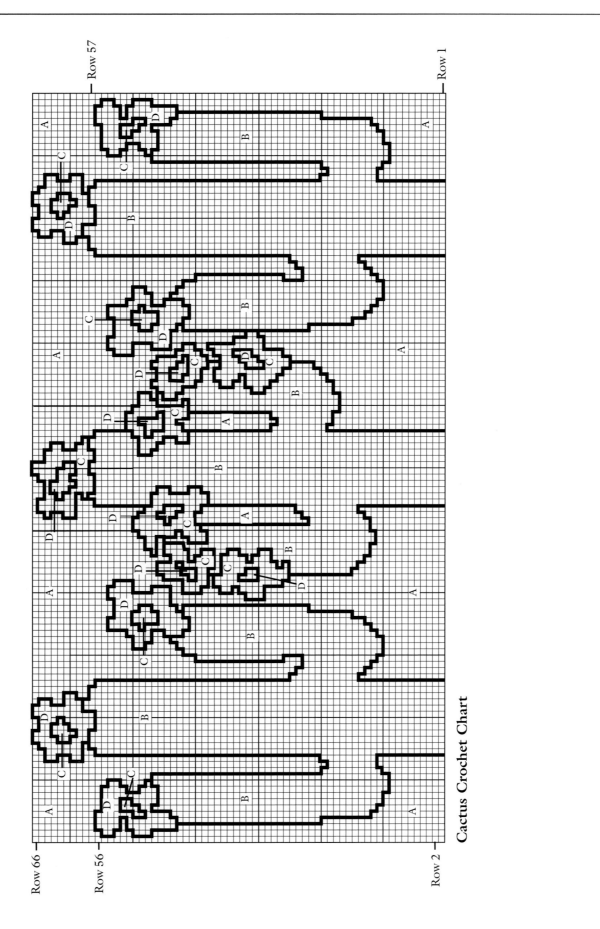

Cactus Crochet Chart

O

Ode to
Santa Fe

Ode to Santa Fe

*Sing a song of Santa Fe with this
bright blanket stitched in desert hues.
A perfect Southwestern accent!*

Finished Size

Approximately 40" x 58"

Materials

Lion Brand Jiffy chunky-weight mohair-look yarn (3 oz., 135-yd. ball): 5 Sienna #143 (A), 4 Turquoise #148 (B), 5 Goldenrod #187 (C)

Size K crochet hook or size to obtain gauge

Gauge

3 hdc and 2½ rows = 1"

Directions

Note: To change colors, work last yo of last st in prev color with new color, dropping prev color to WS of work. Do not carry yarn not in use across the row.

Afghan: With A, ch 111.

Row 1 (RS): Referring to chart for color changes, hdc in 2nd ch from hook and in ea rem ch across, turn = 110 hdc across.

Rows 2 and foll: Ch 1, work in hdc, changing colors according to chart. Read chart from right to left on odd-numbered rows (RS) and left to right on even-numbered rows (WS). Rep Rows 1–48, twice. Rep Rows 1–40 once more. Fasten off all yarns.

Border: Matching yarn color to edge, join yarn with sl st in corner, sc evenly across ea side edge of afghan. Fasten off.

Rnd 1: Join A with sl st in corner, * sc evenly across to next corner, 3 sc in corner, rep from * around, sl st in first sc.

Rnds 2–6: Ch 1, * sc in ea st to center corner st, 3 sc in corner st, rep from * around, sl st in first sc. Fasten off after last rnd.

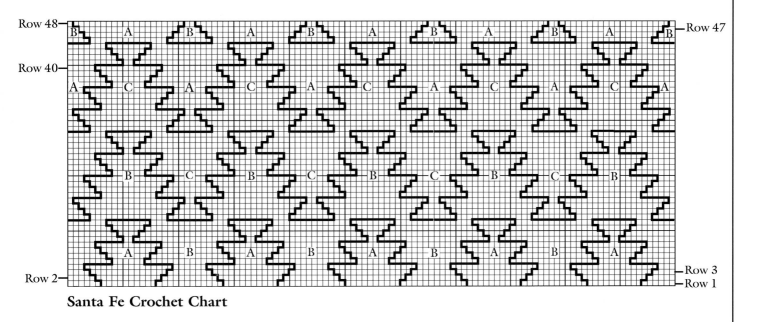

Santa Fe Crochet Chart

O

October
Afternoon

October Afternoon

*When fall winds blow, cuddle up
in this quilt-like afghan of burgundy, taupe,
and deep forest green.*

Finished Size

Approximately 43" x 59"

Materials

Lion Brand Jiffy Chunky bulky-weight yarn
(3 oz., 120-yd. ball): 1 Taupe #125 (A), 2 Country Green #181 (B), 3 Sienna #143 (C), 4 Forest
Green #131 (D), 6 Burgundy #142 (E)

Size K crochet hook or size to obtain gauge

Gauge

Square = 8"

Directions

Note: To change colors, work last yo of last st in
prev color with new color.

Square (make 35): *Center:* With A, ch 7.

Row 1: Sc in 3rd ch from hook (for first sc and
ch-1 sp), (ch 1, sk 1 ch, sc in next ch) twice, turn.

Row 2: Ch 2 (for first sc and ch-1 sp), sc in first
ch-1 sp, ch 1, sc in next ch-1 sp, ch 1, sc in 2nd ch
of tch, turn.

Rows 3–5: Rep Row 2, changing to B in last st
of Row 5, turn. Fasten off A.

Section B: **Row 1:** With B, ch 2 (for first sc and ch-1 sp), working back across last row of Center, sc in
first ch-1 sp, ch 1, sc in next ch-1 sp, ch 1 (sc, ch 2,
sc) in ch-2 at end of row for corner, working across
side edge of Center, ch 1, sk next row, sc in next
row, ch 1, sc in beg ch of foundation ch-7, turn.

Row 2: Ch 2 (for first sc and ch-1 sp), (sc, ch 1)
in ea ch-1 sp across to corner ch-2 sp, (sc, ch 2, sc)
in corner sp, (ch 1, sc) in ea rem ch-1 sp, ending
with ch 1, sc in 2nd ch of tch, turn.

Rows 3–5: Rep Row 2, changing to C in last st
of Row 5. Do not turn. Fasten off B.

Section C: **Row 1:** With piece turned to work
across row ends of Section B and using C, ch 2 (for
first sc and ch-1 sp), sk first row, (sc in next row, ch

1, sk next row) twice, sc in st at edge of Center, ch
1, (sk 1 ch of foundation ch, sc in next ch, ch 1)
twice, (sc, ch 2, sc) in last st of Center, working
across edge of Center, ch 1, sk next row, sc in next
row, ch 1, sc in last row of Center, working across
row ends of Section B, (ch 1, sk next row, sc in
next row) twice, ch 1, sc in last row of Section B,
turn.

Rows 2–5: Rep Row 2 as for Section B, changing
to D in last st of Row 5. Do not turn. Fasten off C.

Section D: **Row 1:** With piece turned to work
across row ends of Section C and last row of Section B, and using D, ch 2 (for first sc and ch-1 sp),
sk first row, (sc in next row, ch 1, sk next row)
twice, sc in st at edge of next Section, (ch 1, sc in
next ch-1 sp) across to corner ch-2 sp, ch 1, (sc, ch
2, sc) in corner sp, (ch 1, sc in next ch-1 sp) across
to end of Section, ch 1, sc in first row of next Section, ch 1, sk next row, sc in next row, ch 1, sc in
last row of Section, turn.

Rows 2–5: Rep Row 2 as for Section B, changing
to E in last st of Row 5. Do not turn. Fasten off D.

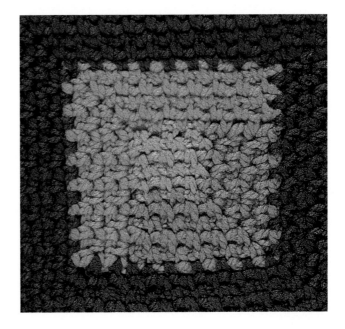

continued on page 84

continued from page 83

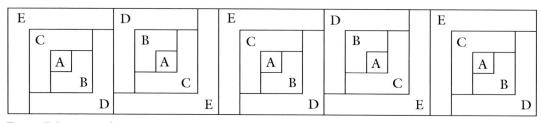

Row Diagram A

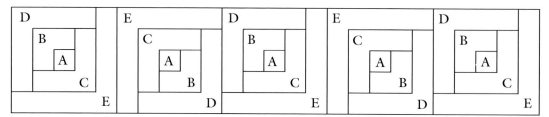

Row Diagram B

Section E: **Row 1:** With piece turned to work across row ends of Section D and last row of Section C, and using E, ch 2 (for first sc and ch-1 sp), work as for Row 1 of Section D.

Rows 2–5: Rep Row 2 as for Section B. Fasten off after last row.

Assembly: Referring to Row Diagram A, whipstitch squares together to make 4 rows. Referring to Row Diagram B, whipstitch squares together to make 3 rows. Whipstitch rows together alternately.

Border: **Rnd 1:** With RS facing, join E with sl st in any corner, ch 3 for first sc and ch 2, sc in same corner, * (ch 1, sc in next ch-1 sp) across to next corner, (sc, ch 2, sc) in corner, rep from * around, end with sl st in first ch of beg ch-3.

Rnds 2–5: Sl st into corner ch-2 sp, ch 3 for first sc and ch 2, sc in same corner, * (ch 1, sc in next ch-1 sp) across to next corner ch-2 sp, (sc, ch 2, sc) in corner sp, rep from * around, end with sl st in first ch of beg ch-3. Fasten off after last rnd.

Perfectly Pink

Perfectly Pink

*Using fun-to-learn filet crochet,
make a throw that combines two of my favorite
things—hearts and the color pink.*

Finished Size

Approximately 35" x 45"

Materials

Lion Brand Jamie Pompadour sportweight yarn
(1.75 oz., 196-yd. skein): 7 Pink #201
Size F crochet hook or size to obtain gauge
8 yards ⅜"-wide pink satin ribbon

Gauge

9 dc and 5 rows = 2"

Filet Crochet Stitches

Block over Block: Dc in ea of next 3 dc.
Space over Space: Ch 2, dc in next dc.
First Block of Row over Block: Ch 3, dc in ea of
next 3 dc.
Block over Space: 2 dc in next ch-2 sp, dc in
next dc.

Space over Block: Ch 2, sk next 2 dc, dc in
next dc.

Directions

Afghan: Ch 168 loosely.

Row 1 (RS): Dc in 4th ch from hook and in ea
of next 2 ch, ch 2, sk next 2 ch, dc in next ch, ch 2,
sk next 2 ch, dc in ea of next 4 ch, * ch 2, sk next 2
ch, (dc in next ch, ch 2, sk next 2 ch) 12 times, dc
in ea of next 4 ch, ch 2, sk next 2 ch, dc in next ch,
ch 2, sk next 2 ch, dc in next 4 ch, rep from *
across, turn = 47 ch-2 sps across.

Row 2 (WS): Ch 3 (for first dc), dc in ea of next
3 dc, ch 2, sl st in next dc, work Space over Space,
work Block over Block, * work Space over Space
13 times, work Block over Block, ch 2, sl st in next
dc, work Space over Space, work Block over Block,
rep from * across, turn.

Row 3: Work First Block of Row over Block, ch
2, tr in sl st, work Space over Space, work Block
over Block, * work Space over Space 13 times,
work Block over Block, ch 2, tr in sl st, work Space
over Space, work Block over Block, rep from *
across, turn.

Row 4: Work First Block of Row over Block, ch
2, sl st in tr, work Space over Space, work Block
over Block, * work Space over Space 6 times, work
Block over Space, work Space over Space 6 times,
work Block over Block, ch 2, sl st in tr, work Space
over Space, work Block over Block, rep from *
across, turn.

Rows 5–17: Cont foll chart as est, rep indicated
portion for pat. Read chart from right to left on
odd-numbered rows (RS) and left to right on
even-numbered rows (WS).

Rows 18–101: Rep Rows 4–17 of chart 6
times.

Row 102: Work First Block of Row
over Block, ch 2, dc in tr, work Space
over Space, work Block over Block,
* work Space over Space 13 times, work
Block over Block, ch 2, dc in tr, work Space

over Space, work Block over Block, rep from *
across, turn. Do not fasten off.

Edging: **Rnd 1** (eyelet rnd): With RS facing, ch 6
(for first dc and ch 3), dc in same st for corner,
working across last row of afghan, ch 1, dc in next
dc, ch 1, (sk 1 st, dc in next st, ch 1) across to last 2
sts of prev row, dc in next dc, (dc, ch 3, dc) in last
dc for corner, * ch 1, working in ends of rows
across side edge of afghan, (dc in top of dc on next
row, ch 1) across to corner **, working in free lps
of foundation ch, (dc, ch 3, dc) in first ch for corner, ch 1, dc in next ch, ch 1, (sk next ch, dc in
next ch, ch 1) across to last 2 ch, dc in next ch, (dc,
ch 3, dc) in last ch for corner, rep from * to **
once more, sl st in 3rd ch of beg ch-6 = 368 ch-1
sps around.

   Rnd 2: Ch 5 (for first dc and ch 2), dc in same
st, ch 2, (dc, ch 2) 4 times in corner ch-3 sp, * (dc,
ch 2, dc) in next dc (V-st made), [dc in next dc, ch

2, V-st in next dc] across to dc before corner ch-3
sp, ch 2, V-st in next dc, ch 2, (dc, ch 2) 4 times in
corner ch-3 sp, rep from * around, end with sl st in
3rd ch of beg ch-5.

   Rnd 3: Sl st into first ch-2 sp, ch 5 (for first dc
and ch 2), (dc in next ch-2 sp, ch 2) around, sl st in
3rd ch of beg ch-5.

   Rnd 4: Ch 5 (for first dc and ch 2), (dc in next
dc, ch 2) around, sl st in 3rd ch of beg ch-5.

   Rnd 5: Sl st into first ch-2 sp, ch 3, (sl st in next
ch-2 sp, ch 3) around, sl st in first sl st. Fasten off.

Finishing: From ribbon, cut 2 (64") lengths and
2 (76") lengths. Weave 64" ribbons through eyelet round at short ends of afghan, leaving 12" tails
at each corner of afghan. In same manner, weave
76" ribbons through eyelet rnd at side edges of
afghan, leaving tails at corners. Tie ribbon tails
into bows at corners and trim streamers.

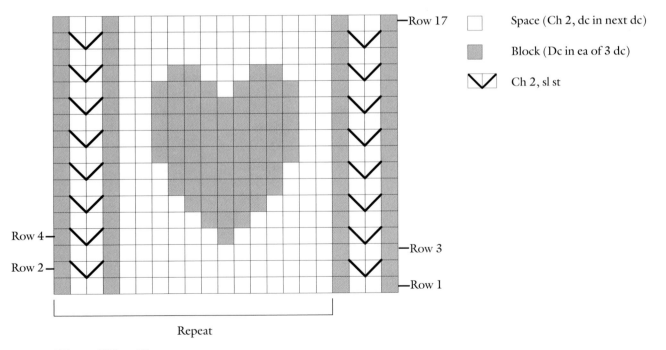

Heart Filet Chart

Pretty
Baskets

Pretty Baskets

*I like the simplicity of this attractive pattern.
The woven effect will complement
many different settings.*

Finished Size

Approximately 38¾" x 54"

Materials

Lion Brand Keepsake Sayelle* worsted-weight yarn (6 oz., 312-yd. skein): 9 Sage #132

Size K crochet hook or size to obtain gauge

Gauge

14 sts = 4"

1 pat rep (22 rows) = 8"

Pattern Stitches

Front Post DC (FPdc): (See page 141.) Yo, insert hook from front to back to front around the post (upright portion of the dc st) of the indicated st on the row below, yo and pull up a lp even with last st (or beg ch) made, (yo and pull through 2 lps on hook) twice = 1 FPdc made. Sk 1 st behind ea FPdc.

Back Post DC (BPdc): Yo, insert hook from back to front to back around the post (upright portion of the dc st) of the indicated st on the row below, yo and pull up a lp even with last st (or beg ch) made, (yo and pull through 2 lps on hook) twice = 1 BPdc made. Sk 1 st behind ea BPdc.

Directions

Afghan: Ch 130 loosely.

Row 1 (WS): Dc in 4th ch from hook and in ea rem ch across, turn = 128 dc across.

Row 2 (RS): Ch 2, 1 FPdc around post of ea of next 14 sts, (1 BPdc around post of ea of next 14 sts, 1 FPdc around post of ea of next 14 sts) 4 times, dc in top of tch, turn.

Row 3: Ch 2, 1 BPdc around post of ea of next 14 sts, (1 FPdc around post of ea of next 14 sts, 1 BPdc around post of ea of next 14 sts) 4 times, dc in top of tch, turn.

Rows 4–11: Rep Rows 2 and 3 alternately.

Row 12: Rep Row 3.

Rows 13–21: Rep Rows 2 and 3 alternately.

Row 22: Rep Row 2.

Rep Rows 2–21, 5 times.

Rep Rows 2–11 once. Fasten off after last row.

Border: **Rnd 1:** With RS facing, join yarn with sl st in top right corner, work * 102 sc evenly spaced across short edge to next corner, 3 sc in corner, work 130 sc evenly spaced across long edge to next corner, 3 sc in corner, rep from * once more.

Rnd 2: * Sc in ea st to center corner st, 3 sc in corner st, rep from * around.

Rnd 3: * Hdc in next st, (yo and insert hook around post of hdc just made, yo and pull up a lp) 3 times, yo and pull through all 7 lps on hook (puff around hdc post made), ch 1, sk 2 sc, rep from * around, end with sl st in bottom of first puff. Fasten off.

2

Quick and Cozy

Quick and Cozy

You can make it in no time!

Finished Size

Approximately 47" x 57"

Materials

Lion Brand Keepsake Sayelle* worsted-weight yarn (6 oz., 312-yd. skein): 6 Lavender #144 (MC), 3 Purple #147 (A), 1 Fisherman #099 (B)

Size K crochet hook or size to obtain gauge

Gauge

13 sts and 8 rows in pat = 4"

Pattern Stitch

Front Post DC (FPdc): (See page 141.) Yo, insert hook from front to back to front around the post (upright portion of the dc st) of the indicated st on the row below, yo and pull up a lp even with last st made, (yo and pull through 2 lps on hook) twice = 1 FPdc made. Sk 1 st behind ea FPdc.

Directions

Afghan: With MC, ch 186 loosely.

Row 1 (RS): Dc in 4th ch from hook and in ea rem ch across, turn = 184 sts across.

Row 2: Ch 2 (for first hdc), FPdc around post of ea of next 2 dc, sk 1 st behind ea FPdc, * dc in ea of next 2 dc, FPdc around post of ea of next 2 dc, sk 1 st behind ea FPdc, rep from * across, hdc in top of beg ch, turn.

Row 3: Ch 2 (for first hdc), dc in ea of next 2 FPdc, * FPdc around post of ea of next 2 dc, sk 1 st behind ea FPdc, dc in ea of next 2 FPdc, rep from * across, hdc in top of tch, turn.

Row 4: Ch 2 (for first hdc), FPdc around post of ea of next 2 dc, sk 1 st behind ea FPdc, * dc in ea of next 2 FPdc, FPdc around post of ea of next 2 dc, sk 1 st behind ea FPdc, rep from * across, hdc in top of tch.

Rep Rows 3 and 4 alternately, changing colors as foll: work * 6 rows MC, 4 rows A, 2 rows MC, 4 rows A, 6 rows MC **, 2 rows B, rep from * 3 times more, ending last rep at ** for a total of 94 rows. Fasten off.

Fringe: For each tassel, referring to page 141, cut 5 (18") lengths of yarn. Knot 1 tassel in every other row across each short end of afghan.

2
Quiet
Moments

Quiet Moments

These triangles remind me of kites in a windy sky. I look forward to flying kites on the beach with my son when he is older.

Finished Size

Approximately 44" x 64"

Materials

Lion Brand Jiffy chunky-weight mohair-look yarn: 9 (2.5 oz., 115-yd. balls) Salem multicolor #330 (MC), 5 (3 oz., 135-yd. balls) Lilac #144 (CC1), 4 (3 oz., 135-yd. balls) Rose #140 (CC2)

Size K crochet hook or size to obtain gauge

Gauge

3 hdc = 1"
Square = 10"

Directions

Note: To change colors, work last yo of last st in prev color with new color, dropping prev color to WS of work. Do not carry yarn not in use across the row.

Square: Make 12 with Salem (MC) and Lilac (CC1). Make 12 with Salem (MC) and Rose (CC2).

Row 1 (RS): With MC, ch 32, hdc in 3rd ch from hook and in ea rem ch across, turn = 30 hdc across.

Row 2: Drop MC, join CC, ch 2 (for first hdc), drop CC, pick up MC and hdc in ea rem st across, turn = 30 sts across.

Row 3: With MC, ch 2 (for first hdc), hdc in ea of next 27 sts, drop MC, pick up CC and hdc in ea of 2 rem sts, turn.

Row 4: With CC, ch 2 (for first hdc), hdc in ea of next 3 sts, drop CC, pick up MC and hdc in ea rem st across, turn.

Cont working in hdc as est, changing colors as specified below.

Rows 5 and 6: Work 1 more st with CC and 1 fewer st with MC ea row.

Row 7: Work 2 more sts with CC and 2 fewer sts with MC.

Rows 8–22: Rep Rows 5–7, 4 times = 26 sts CC and 4 sts MC after Row 22.

Row 23: Rep Row 5. Fasten off MC .

Row 24: With CC, ch 2, hdc in ea st across. Fasten off.

Assembly: Referring to Placement Diagram, whip-stitch squares together.

Border: Matching yarn color to edge, join yarn with sl st in corner, sc evenly across ea side edge of afghan. Fasten off.

Rnd 1: Join CC1 with sl st in any corner, * sc evenly across to next corner, 3 sc in corner, rep from * around, sl st in first sc.

Rnd 2: * Sc in ea st to center corner st, 3 sc in corner st, rep from * around, sl st in first sc. Fasten off CC1.

Rnd 3: Join MC, rep Rnd 2. Fasten off MC.

Rnds 4 and 5: Join CC1, rep Rnd 2. Fasten off after last rnd.

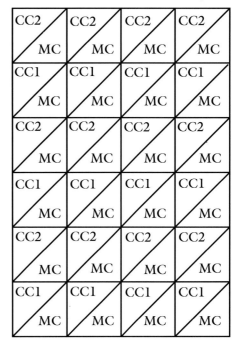

Placement Diagram

R

Radio Waves

Radio Waves

Crochet this classic while tuning in to your favorite music. Be sure to count stitches carefully for even ripples!

Finished Size

Approximately 56" x 70"

Materials

Lion Brand Keepsake Sayelle* worsted-weight yarn (6 oz., 312-yd. skein): 7 Fisherman #099 (MC); 2 each Dark Brown #127 (A), Cocoa Brown #123 (B), Pine #182 (C)

Size H crochet hook or size to obtain gauge

Gauge

26 sts in pat = 7"
4 rows in pat = 2"

Directions

Afghan: With MC, ch 209 loosely.

Row 1 (WS): Sc in 2nd ch from hook and in ea of next 5 ch, 3 sc in next ch, * sc in ea of next 5 ch, sk next 2 ch, sc in ea of next 5 ch, 3 sc in next ch, rep from * across to last 6 ch, sc in ea of last 6 ch, turn = 210 sc across.

Row 2 (RS): Ch 3 (for first dc), sk next sc, dc in ea of next 5 sc, 3 dc in next sc (center st of 3-sc grp), dc in ea of next 5 sc, * sk next 2 sc, dc in ea of next 5 sc, 3 dc in next sc, dc in ea of next 5 sc, rep from * across to last 2 sc, sk next sc, dc in last sc. Fasten off.

Row 3: With WS facing, join next color (see color sequence below) with sl st in first st, ch 1, sc in same st as tch, sk next dc, sc in ea of next 5 dc, 3 sc in next dc (center st of 3-dc grp), sc in ea of next 5 dc, * sk next 2 dc, sc in ea of next 5 dc, 3 sc in next dc, sc in ea of next 5 dc, rep from * across to last 2 dc, sk next dc, sc in top of tch, turn = 210 sc across.

Rep Rows 2 and 3 alternately until piece measures 70" from beg, working color in the foll sequence: 2 rows A, 2 rows MC, 2 rows B, 2 rows MC, 2 rows C, 2 rows MC, ending after last rep of Row 2 with MC. Fasten off.

Fringe: For each tassel, referring to page 141 of General Directions, cut 2 (20") lengths of MC. Knot 1 tassel in each stitch across each short end of afghan.

R

Rainbow Treasure

Rainbow Treasure

*Looking for treasure at the end
of the rainbow? Finish this afghan and
you'll have your treasure!*

Finished Size

Approximately 46" x 68"

Materials

Lion Brand Jiffy chunky-weight mohair-look yarn (3 oz., 135-yd. ball): 4 Mint #156 (A); 3 each Light Pink #101 (B), Pastel Blue #105 (C), Melon #184 (D), Pastel Yellow #157 (E)

Size K crochet hook or size to obtain gauge

Gauge

5 dc and 3 rows = 2"

Directions

Afghan: With A, ch 107 loosely.

Row 1 (WS): Dc in 4th ch from hook and in ea rem ch across, turn = 105 dc across.

Rows 2–10: Ch 3 (for first dc), dc in ea dc across, end with dc in top of tch = about 6" from beg. Fasten off A.

Join next color and rep Row 2 to work 10 rows ea in dc with B, C, D, E, A, B, C, D, E. Fasten off.

Border: **Row 1:** With RS facing and afghan turned to work across side edge, join A with sl st in bottom right corner of afghan, ch 3 (for first dc), dc evenly across to next corner, 5 dc in corner, dc bet 2 dc across top edge, 5 dc in corner, dc evenly across side edge to next bottom corner, turn.

Rows 2 and 3: Ch 3 (for first dc), dc bet 2 dc around to opposite bottom corner of afghan, turn.

Row 4: Ch 3 (for first dc), (dc bet 2 dc to corner, 2 dc bet 2 dc in ea of 3 center sps at top corner) twice, dc bet 2 dc to bottom corner. Fasten off.

Fringe: For each tassel, referring to page 141 of General Directions, cut 2 (6") lengths of yarn. Referring to photo and knotting 1 tassel in every other stitch, make 1 row of fringe with B across last row of first A section. Make additional rows of fringe on last row of each section, using yarn color of next section.

Terms and Techniques

In making this afghan, you'll learn two important crochet basics: working stripes of color and making fringe.

Working stripes: Many patterns are built with bands of alternating colors. Practice keeping careful count of your rows so that each band of color will be the same width.

Making fringe: Fringe is a welcome accent in many afghan designs—and it's fun to do! Turn to page 141 of General Directions for complete fringe how-tos.

Stained
Glass

Stained Glass

*This afghan, worked in rich chenille,
reminds me of the beautiful stained glass
in my church when I was young.*

Finished Size

Approxmately 51" x 68"

Materials

Lion Brand Chenille worsted-weight chenille yarn (1.4 oz., 87-yd. skein): 7 each Forest Green #131, Royal Blue #109, Red #112, Orange #133, Brown #126; 8 Mulberry #142; 9 Evergreen #130

Size H crochet hook or size to obtain gauge

Gauge

Square = 3"

Pattern Stitch

Puff st: (Yo, insert hook where indicated, yo and pull up a lp) 4 times, yo and pull through all 9 lps on hook, ch 1 to complete puff st.

Directions

Square: Make 357 total. Make 60 squares ea with Royal Blue, Red, and Mulberry; make 59 squares ea with Orange, Brown, and Evergreen. Use Forest Green for joining and border.

Ch 5, join with sl st to form a ring.

Rnd 1: Ch 1, (puff st in ring, ch 1) 8 times, sl st in top of first puff st = 8 puff sts around.

Rnd 2: Sl st in first ch-1 sp, ch 1, (puff st, ch 1) twice in same sp, * puff st in next sp, ch 1, (puff st, ch 1) twice in next sp, rep from * around, sl st in top of first puff st = 12 puff sts around.

Rnd 3: Ch 1, sc in same st, * (3 sc, ch 1, 3 sc) in next sp, (sc in next puff st, 2 sc in next sp) twice, sc in next puff st, rep from * around, sl st in first sc. Fasten off.

Assembly: Refer to Placement Diagram for positioning and arrange colors as desired. With wrong sides facing and using Forest Green, sc squares tog through bk lps only.

Border: **Rnd 1:** With RS facing, join Forest Green with sl st in any corner, sl st in bk lp only of ea st around, sl st in ft lp only of first st.

Rnd 2: Ch 1, sc in ft lp only of same st as sl st, sc in ft lp only of ea st around, sl st in first sc. Fasten off.

Placement Diagram

Shooting Marbles

Shooting Marbles

*As a kid, I was considered one of the best
marble shooters in the neighborhood.
I had socks full of marbles!*

Finished Size

Approximately 37" x 48"

Materials

Lion Brand Jiffy chunky-weight mohair-look
yarn (3 oz., 135-yd. ball): 4 Goldenrod #187; 1
each Scarlet #113, Turquoise #148, Heather Blue
#111, Evergreen #130, Lilac #144, Mulberry
#190, Rose #140; 5 Pastel Yellow #157
Size K crochet hook or size to obtain gauge

Gauge

Hexagon = 5"

Directions

Hexagon: Make 86 total. **For Rnd 1:** Use Goldenrod on all hexagons. **For Rnd 2:** Make 12 hexagons ea with Scarlet, Turquoise, Heather Blue,
Evergreen, and Lilac; make 13 hexagons ea with
Mulberry and Rose. **For Rnd 3:** Use Pastel Yellow
on all hexagons.

With Goldenrod, ch 6, join with sl st to form a
ring.

Rnd 1: Ch 3 (for first dc), dc in ring, ch 2, (2 dc
in ring, ch 2) 5 times, sl st in top of beg ch-3 = 12
dc and 6 ch-2 sps around. Fasten off.

Rnd 2: Join next color with sl st in any ch-2 sp,
ch 3 (for first dc), (dc, ch 2, 2 dc) in same sp, * (2
dc, ch 2, 2 dc) in next sp, rep from * 4 times more,
sl st in top of beg ch-3. Fasten off.

Rnd 3: Join Pastel Yellow with sl st in any ch-2 sp,
ch 3 (for first dc), (dc, ch 2, 2 dc) in same sp, * dc in
ea of next 4 dc, (2 dc, ch 2, 2 dc) in next sp, rep
from * around, sl st in top of beg ch-3. Fasten off.

Assembly: Referring to Placement Diagram and
working through back loops only, whipstitch
hexagons together, arranging colors as desired.

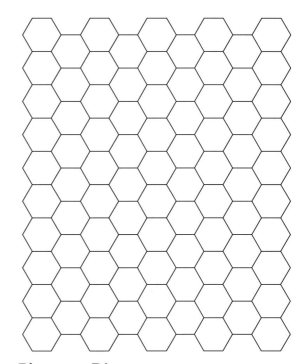

Placement Diagram

T

*Tea
Time*

Tea Time

Shouldn't we all take time out for a spot of tea in the afternoon? Make mine a nice herbal tea.

Finished Size

Approximately 44" x 66"

Materials

Lion Brand Jiffy chunky-weight mohair-look yarn (3 oz., 135-yd. ball): 12 Navy #110; 3 White #100; 1 each Pastel Yellow #157, Light Pink #101

Size J afghan and crochet hooks or size to obtain gauge

Large-eyed tapestry needle

Assorted ribbons, lace, ribbon roses, beads, and fabric scraps for embellishment

Gauge

13 sts and 11 rows = 4" in afghan st
Block = 18" x 20"

Directions

Note: See page 140 for afghan st directions.

Block (make 6): With Navy and afghan hook, ch 64, work 53 rows afghan st. Sl st in ea vertical bar across. Fasten off.

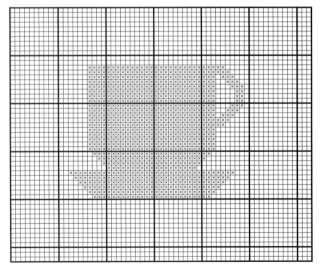

Cross-stitch Chart

continued on page 104

continued from page 103

Border: With RS facing and crochet hook, join White with sl st in any corner of block, ch 1, * sc evenly across to next corner, 3 sc in corner, rep from * around, sl st in first sc. Fasten off.

Cross-stitch: Using 1 strand of yarn, cross-stitch 1 teacup on each block according to chart (see page 103). Make 2 White teacups, 2 Yellow teacups, and 2 Light Pink teacups.

Referring to photo for inspiration, embellish teacups as desired.

Assembly: Afghan is 2 blocks wide and 3 blocks long. Whipstitch blocks together, arranging teacups as desired.

Edging: Rnd 1: With WS facing and crochet hook, join White with sl st in any corner, ch 1, * sc evenly across to next corner, 3 sc in corner, rep from * around, sl st in first sc, turn.

Rnd 2 (RS): Sl st into center st of corner, ch 3 (for first dc), 2 dc in same st, * sk 2 sc, sl st in next sc, sk 2 sc, 5 dc in next sc, rep from * around, end with 2 dc in same st as beg, sl st in top of beg ch-3. Fasten off.

T

*Tickle
the
Ivories*

Tickle the Ivories

*I took piano lessons for six years,
and I would like to dedicate this afghan
to my teacher, Joan Jerdan.*

Finished Size

Approximately 42½" x 52"

Materials

Lion Brand Jamie 4 Kids worsted-weight yarn (2 oz., 140-yd. skein): 7 Fire Engine Red #113 (A); 4 Flag Blue #109 (B); 2 each Shadow Black #153 (C), Snow White #100 (D)

Size J crochet hook or size to obtain gauge

Gauge

6 sc and 7 rows = 2"

Directions

Note: To change colors, work last yo of last st in prev color with new color, dropping prev color to WS of work. Carry yarn not in use loosely across the row.

Musical notes are crocheted separately and stitched to completed afghan.

Afghan: With A, ch 121 loosely.

Row 1 (RS): Sc in 2nd ch from hook and in ea rem ch across, turn = 120 sc across.

Rows 2–113: Ch 1, work in sc, changing colors according to chart. Read chart from right to left on odd-numbered rows (RS) and left to right on even-numbered rows (WS).

Rows 114 and foll: Referring to chart, rep Rows 2–68 once.

Last Row: With A, sc in ea st across. Fasten off all yarns.

Border: **Rnd 1:** With RS facing, join A with sl st in any corner, * sc evenly across to next corner, 3 sc in corner, rep from * around, sl st in first sc.

Rnds 2–5: Ch 1, * sc in ea st to center corner st, 3 sc in corner st, rep from * around, sl st in first sc. Fasten off after last rnd.

Musical Notes: For each note, using C, crochet a ch 12" long. Fasten off. Spiral 1 end of ch into a circle. Referring to photo, stitch notes to afghan. For joining bars, using C, crochet a ch of required length and stitch to afghan.

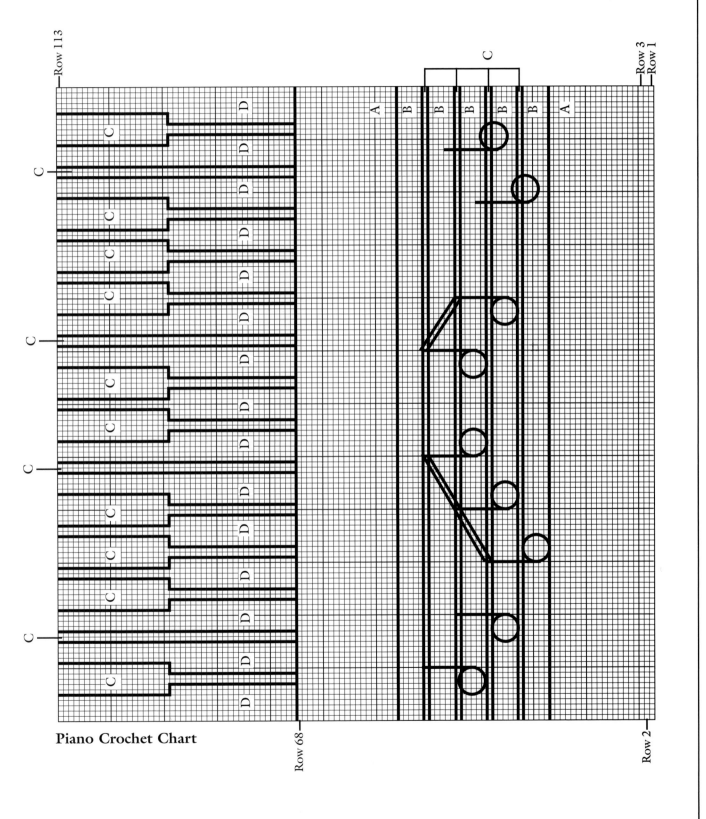

Piano Crochet Chart

U
*Under
the
Mulberry
Tree*

Under the Mulberry Tree

This cozy wrap makes up quickly.
You may also want to try making it
in a lovely solid color.

Finished Size

Approximately 46" x 62"

Materials

Lion Brand Jiffy chunky-weight mohair-look yarn (2.5 oz., 115-yd. ball): 27 San Antonio multicolor #327

Size N crochet hook or size to obtain gauge

Gauge

10 dc and 5 rows = 4"

Directions

Afghan: With 2 strands of yarn held tog as 1, ch 117 loosely.

Row 1 (RS): Dc in 4th ch from hook and in ea of next 4 ch, ch 1, sk next ch, * dc in ea of next 5 ch, ch 1, sk next ch, rep from * across to last 6 ch, dc in ea of last 6 ch, turn.

Row 2: Ch 3 (for first dc), dc in same st, ch 2, sk next 2 dc, sc in next dc, * ch 2, 3 dc in next ch-1 sp, ch 2, sk next 2 dc, sc in next dc, rep from * across, ch 2, sk next 2 dc, 2 dc in last dc, turn.

Row 3: Ch 3 (for first dc), dc in next dc and in first ch-2 sp, ch 1, dc in next ch-2 sp, * dc in ea of next 3 dc, dc in next ch-2 sp, ch 1, dc in next ch-2 sp, rep from * across, dc in ea of last 2 dc, turn.

Row 4: Ch 1, sc in first dc, * ch 2, 3 dc in next ch-1 sp, ch 2, sk next 2 dc, sc in next dc, rep from * across, turn.

Row 5: Ch 3 (for first dc), dc in first ch-2 sp, dc in ea of next 3 dc, dc in next ch-2 sp, * ch 1, dc in next ch-2 sp, dc in ea of next 3 dc, dc in next ch-2 sp, rep from * across, dc in last sc, turn.

Rep Rows 2–5 for pat until piece measures approximately 62" from beg, ending after last rep of Row 5. Do not fasten off.

Border: With RS facing, ch 1, * sc evenly across to next corner, 3 sc in corner, rep from * around, sl st in first sc. Fasten off.

Fringe: For each tassel, referring to page 141 of General Directions, cut 2 (18") lengths of yarn. Knot 1 tassel in every other stitch across each short end of afghan.

Terms and Techniques

This afghan is a good example of a pattern that calls for working with two strands of yarn. Simply use two skeins and hold both strands of yarn together, working them as if they were one strand.

This afghan is made with a multicolored yarn. Using two different solid-color yarns would give a different type of multicolored effect. And using two strands of the same solid color is another option for this pattern.

U

Utter
Elegance

Utter Elegance

This afghan works up nicely into a dense, warm fabric that is perfect for long winter nights.

Finished Size

Approximately 43" x 59"

Materials

Lion Brand Jiffy chunky-weight mohair-look yarn (3 oz., 135-yd. ball): 8 each Violet #191, Forest Green #131, Black #153

Sizes N and Q crochet hooks or size to obtain gauge

Gauge

Square = 8" with size Q hook

Directions

Square (make 35): *Note:* Work all rows with RS facing, working odd-numbered rows from right to left and even-numbered rows from left to right.

With 3 strands of yarn (1 strand of ea color) held tog as 1 and size Q hook, ch 14.

Row 1 (RS): Dc in 4th ch from hook and in ea rem ch across = 12 dc across. Do not turn.

Row 2 (RS): Ch 1, working from left to right, sc in ft lp only of last dc of prev row and ea dc across, end with sl st in top of tch = 11 sc across. Do not turn.

Row 3: Ch 3 (for first dc), dc in bk lp only of next st and ea st across to last st of row, sk last st = 11 dc across. Do not turn.

Rep Rows 2 and 3 alternately until piece measures 8" from beg, ending after last rep of Row 3. Fasten off.

Assembly: Afghan is 5 squares wide and 7 squares long. Arrange squares in checkerboard pattern, rotating every other square a quarter turn, so that stitch patterns are at right angles. Whipstitch squares together through front loops only.

Border: **Rnd 1:** With RS facing, size N hook, and 3 strands of yarn (1 strand of ea color) held tog as 1, join yarn with sl st in any corner, * 3 sc in corner, sc in ea st across to next corner, rep from * around, sl st in first sc.

Rnds 2 and 3: * Sc in ea st to center corner st, 3 sc in corner st, rep from * around, sl st in first sc. Fasten off after last rnd.

Terms and Techniques

The afghan just before this one (*Under the Mulberry Tree*) is worked with two strands of yarn. In *Utter Elegance*, we work with three strands! Just hold the three strands (in this case, one each of three different colors) together and work them as if they were one strand. As a result, the piece works up quickly into a thick, cozy texture.

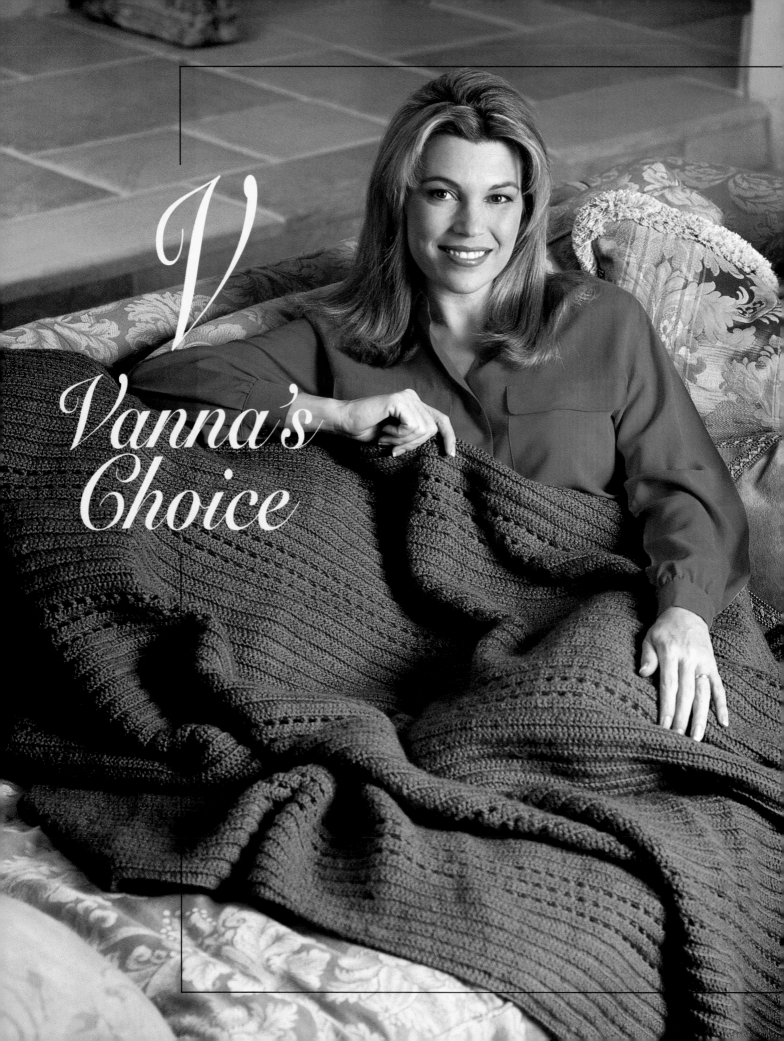

V
Vanna's Choice

Vanna's Choice

If you're new to crochet, let me recommend this tried-and-true pattern. Follow the easy directions for either an adult- or baby-sized throw.

Finished Size

Adult Throw: 49" x 58"
Baby Throw: 24" x 28" (not pictured)

Materials

Lion Brand Jiffy chunky-weight mohair-look yarn (3 oz., 135-yd. ball): 20 Teal #178 for adult throw or 10 for baby throw
Size G crochet hook or size to obtain gauge

Gauge

5 dc = 1"
4 rows = 1¾"

Directions

Note: Directions given are for Adult Throw. Changes for Baby Throw are given in brackets.
***Throw:* DC Band: Row 1** (RS): Ch 291 [141], dc in 4th ch from hook and in ea ch across, turn = 289 [139] dc across.

Row 2: Ch 2 (for first dc), working in bk lps only, dc in ea dc across, turn.

Rep Row 2, 10 [2] times = 12 [4] dc rows.

Mesh Band: Row 1: Ch 5 (for first dc and ch 2), sk 2 dc, dc in next dc, * ch 2, sk 2 dc, dc in next dc, rep from * across, turn.

Row 2: Ch 2 (for first dc), working in bk lps only, * dc in ea ch of ch-2 sp, dc in next dc, rep from * across, turn.

Rows 3–6: Rep Rows 1 and 2 alternately.
Rep Row 2 of DC Band for 12 [4] rows.
Rep Rows 1–6 of Mesh Band.
Cont as est until there are 6 Mesh Bands and 7 DC Bands. Fasten off.

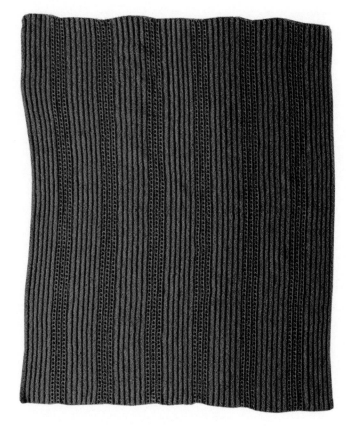

V

Victorian Lace

Victorian Lace

Patterns like this bring back fond memories of my grandmother's crochet. This is an advanced pattern, recommended for experienced crocheters.

Finished Size

Approximately 45" x 51"

Materials

Lion Brand Jamie Pompadour sportweight yarn (1.75 oz., 196-yd. skein): 11 White #200
Size I crochet hook or size to obtain gauge

Gauge

Square = 10½"

Pattern Stitches

Cluster (cl): * Yo 3 times, insert hook where indicated, yo and draw up a lp, (yo and pull through 2 lps on hook) 3 times (2 lps rem on hook), rep from * once more (for 2-dtr cl), [rep from * twice more for 3-dtr cl], yo and pull through all rem lps on hook to complete cl.

Triple crochet st (tr): Yo hook twice, insert hook where indicated, (yo and pull through 2 lps on hook) 3 times. (See General Directions, page 139.)

Double triple (dtr): Yo 3 times, insert hook where indicated, (yo and pull through 2 lps on hook) 4 times.

Triple triple (tr tr): Yo 4 times, insert hook where indicated, (yo and pull through 2 lps on hook) 5 times.

Quadruple triple (quad tr): Yo 5 times, insert hook where indicated, (yo and pull through 2 lps on hook) 6 times.

Quintuple triple (quin tr): Yo 6 times, insert hook where indicated, (yo and pull through 2 lps on hook) 7 times.

Directions

Square (make 16): Ch 16, join with sl st to form a ring.

Rnd 1 (RS): Ch 1, 24 sc in ring, sl st in first sc = 24 sts around.

Rnd 2: Ch 1, sc in same st as sl st, * ch 4, work 2-dtr cl in ea of next 2 sts, work 3 leaves in top of cl just made as foll: ch 7, quad tr in cl, ch 7, sc in cl (first leaf), ch 8, quin tr in cl, ch 8, sc in cl (2nd leaf), ch 7, quad tr in cl, ch 7, sl st in top of same cl (3rd leaf), ch 4, sc in next Rnd-1 sc, ch 7, sk 2 sc, sc in next sc, rep from * 3 times more, sl st in first sc. Fasten off.

Rnd 3: Join yarn with sl st in top of ch-8 before quin tr on center leaf of next 3-leaf grp, ch 1, * sc in top of ch-8, ch 2, sk quin tr, sc in top of next ch-8, ch 5, sc in top of first ch-7 on next leaf, sk quad tr, sc in top of next ch-7, ch 7, sc in top of next ch-7 on next 3-leaf grp, sk quad tr, sc in top of next ch-7, ch 5, rep from * around, sl st in first sc.

Rnd 4: Ch 1, sc in same st as sl st, * 3 sc in next ch-2 sp for corner, sc in next sc, sc in ea ch of next ch-5 sp, sc in ea of next 2 sc, sc in ea ch of next ch-7 sp, sc in ea of next 2 sc, sc in ea ch of next ch-5 sp, sc in next sc, rep from * around, end with sl st in first sc.

Rnd 5: Sl st into center corner st, ch 4 (for first dc and ch 1), dc in same st as sl st, * (ch 1, sk 1 sc, dc in next sc) across to center corner st, (ch 1, dc) 3 times in corner st, rep from * around, end with dc in beg corner, ch 1, sl st in 3rd ch of beg ch-4.

Rnd 6: Ch 4 (for first dc and ch 1), dc in same st as sl st, * (ch 1, dc in next ch-1 sp) across to center corner st, (ch 1, dc) 3 times in corner st, rep from * around, ending with dc in beg corner, ch 1, sl st in 3rd ch of beg ch-4.

Rnd 7: Ch 3 (for first dc), dc in same st as sl st, * ch 1, (dc in next ch-1 sp, dc in next dc, ch 1, sk next ch-1 sp, dc in next dc, dc in next ch-1 sp, ch 1, sk 1 dc) 5 times, dc in next ch-1 sp, dc in next dc, ch 1, sk next ch-1 sp, dc in next dc, dc in next ch-1 sp, ch 1, 3 dc in center corner st, rep from * around, ending with dc in beg corner, sl st in top of beg ch-3.

Rnd 8: Ch 4 (for first dc and ch 1), dc in same st as sl st, * dc in next dc, (ch 1, sk ch-1 sp, dc in ea of next 2 dc) across to center corner st, (ch 1, dc) 3 times in corner st, rep from * around, end with dc in beg corner, ch 1, sl st in 3rd ch of beg ch-4.

continued on page 116

continued from page 115

Rnd 9: Ch 1, 2 sc in same st as sl st, * sc in ea ch-1 sp and dc across to center corner st, 3 sc in corner st, rep from * around, end with sc in beg corner, sl st in first sc.

Rnd 10: Ch 5, work 2-dtr cl in same st as sl st, ch 2, work 3-dtr cl in same st, * ch 5, sk 4 sc, work 3-dtr cl in next sc, (ch 5, sk 5 sc, work 3-dtr cl in next sc) 6 times, ch 5, sk 4 sc, (3-dtr cl, ch 2, 3-dtr cl) in center corner st, rep from * around, end with ch 5, sk last 4 sc, sl st in top of first cl.

Rnd 11: Ch 1, * sc in ea ch and in ea cl across to next corner sp, 3 sc in corner ch-2 sp, rep from * around, sl st in first sc. Fasten off.

Assembly: Whipstitch squares together in 4 strips of 4 each.

Joining Band: With RS facing and strip turned to work across long edge, join yarn with sl st in corner.

Row 1: Ch 3 (for first dc), work 210 dc evenly spaced across to end of strip, turn.

Row 2: Ch 5 (for first dc and ch 2), sk 3 dc, * dc in next dc, ch 2, sk 2 dc, rep from * across, end with dc in top of tch, turn.

Row 3: Ch 3 (for first dc), * 2 dc in ch-2 sp, dc in next dc, rep from * across, end with dc in 3rd ch of tch, turn.

Rows 4 and 5: Rep Rows 2 and 3. Fasten off after Row 5.

Rep to work Joining Band on 1 long edge of ea of 2 more strips. Whipstitch strips together aligning joining band edge with unworked edge of next strip.

Border: **Rnd 1:** With RS facing and afghan turned to work across top edge, join yarn with sl st in corner, ch 3 (for first dc), * work 210 dc evenly spaced across to next corner, 3 dc in corner, 240 dc evenly spaced across to next corner, 3 dc in corner, rep from * once more, end with 2 dc in beg corner, sl st in top of beg ch-3.

Rnd 2: Ch 4 (for first dc and ch 1), sk 1 dc, dc in next dc, * (ch 1, sk 1 dc, dc in next dc) to next corner, (ch 1, dc) 3 times in center corner st, rep from * around, sl st in 3rd ch of beg ch-4.

Rnd 3: Ch 1, sc in same st as sl st, sc in next ch-1 sp, * sk 1 dc, 5 dc in next sp (shell made), sk 1 dc, sc in next ch-1 sp, sc in next dc, sc in next ch-1 sp, rep from * around, sl st in first sc. Fasten off.

W

Winter Wonderland

Winter Wonderland

*This will put you in the spirit of winter.
The hexagons are easy to work and are
a fun change from plain squares.*

Finished Size

Approximately 52" x 74"

Materials

Lion Brand Keepsake Sayelle* worsted-weight yarn (6 oz., 312-yd. skein): 7 White #100 (MC), 4 Royal Blue #109 (CC).

Size I crochet hook or size to obtain gauge

Gauge

Hexagon = 6½" across

Directions

Hexagon (make 98): **Rnd 1** (RS): With MC, ch 4, 11 dc in 4th ch from hook, sl st in top of beg ch-4 = 12 dc around.

Rnd 2: Ch 6 (for first dc and ch 3), dc in same st, ch 1, sk next dc, * (dc, ch 3, dc) in next dc, ch 1, sk next dc, rep from * around, sl st in 3rd ch of beg ch-6 = 6 ch-3 sps around.

Rnd 3: Sl st into first sp, ch 3 (for first dc), (2 dc, ch 2, 3 dc) in same sp, ch 1, * (3 dc, ch 2, 3 dc) in next ch-3 sp, ch 1, rep from * around, sl st in top of beg ch-3. Fasten off.

Rnd 4: With RS facing, join CC with sc in first st of prev rnd, * ch 1, sk next dc, sc in next dc, ch 3, sc in next dc, ch 1, sk next dc, sc in next dc, working in front of next ch-1 sp, tr in rnd-2 ch-1 sp below next ch-1 sp **, sc in next dc, rep from * 5 times more, ending last rep at **, sl st in first sc.

Rnd 5: Ch 1, sc in same st, * ch 1, dc in next sc, ch 1, (dc, ch 1, tr, ch 1, dc) in next ch-3 sp, ch 1, dc in next sc, ch 1, sc in next sc, ch 1, sk next tr **, sc in next sc, rep from * 5 times more, ending last rep at **, sl st in first sc. Fasten off.

Rnd 6: With RS facing, join MC with sc in ch-1 sp to right of any tr, * ch 3, sc in next ch-1 sp, ch 2, dc in next ch-1 sp, ch 1, [yo twice, pull up a lp in next ch-1 sp, (yo and pull through 2 lps on hook) twice] 3 times, yo and pull through all 4 lps on hook (dec made), ch 1, dc in next ch-1 sp, ch 2 **, sc in next ch-1 sp, rep from * 5 times more, ending

last rep at **, sl st in first sc. Fasten off.

Half-Hexagon (make 12): **Row 1** (RS): With MC, ch 4, 6 dc in 4th ch from hook, turn = 7 dc across.

Row 2: Ch 4, dc in same st, [ch 1, sk next dc, (dc, ch 3, dc) in next dc] twice, ch 1, sk next dc, (dc, ch 1, sc) in last st, turn.

Row 3: Ch 3, 2 dc in first ch-1 sp, [ch 1, (3 dc, ch 2, 3 dc) in next ch-3 sp] twice, ch 1, sk next ch-1 sp, 3 dc in last sp. Fasten off.

Row 4: With RS facing, join CC with sc in top of beg ch, * ch 1, sk next dc, sc in next dc, working in front of next ch-1 sp, tr in row-2 ch-1 sp below next ch-1 sp, sc in next dc, ch 1, sk next dc, sc in next dc **, ch 3, sc in next dc, rep from * twice more, ending last rep at **, turn.

Row 5: Ch 4, (dc, ch 1, dc) in same st, * ch 1, sc in next sc, ch 1, sk next tr, sc in next sc, ch 1 **, dc in next sc, ch 1, (dc, ch 1, tr, ch 1, dc) in next ch-3 sp, ch 1, dc in next sc, rep from * twice more, ending last rep at **, (dc, ch 1, dc, tr) in last sc. Fasten off.

Row 6: With RS facing, join MC with sc in first tr, ch 2, dc in next ch-1 sp, ch 1, [yo twice, pull up a lp in next ch-1 sp, (yo and pull through 2 lps on hook) twice] 3 times, yo and pull through all 4 lps on hook (dec made), ch 1, dc in next ch-1 sp, ch 2, * sc in next ch-1 sp, ch 3, sc in next ch-1 sp, ch 2, dc in next ch-1 sp, ch 1, [yo twice, pull up a lp in next ch-1 sp, (yo and pull through 2 lps on hook) twice] 3 times, yo and pull through all 4 lps on hook (dec made), ch 1, dc in next ch-1 sp, ch 2, rep from * once more, sc in top of beg ch-4, ch 3, working in end of rows, sl st in first row, ch 1, sk next row, (sl st in next row, ch 1) 3 times, sl st in center sp of motif, (ch 1, sl st in next row) 3 times, ch 1, sk next row, sl st in next row, ch 3, sl st in first sc. Fasten off.

Assembly: Using MC, whipstitch 2 hexagons together from center ch of 1 corner ch-3 sp to center ch of next corner ch-3 sp. Repeat to join pieces into 7 strips of 8 hexagons each and 6 strips of 7 hexagons each. Whipstitch strips together alternately. Whipstitch half-hexagons in place along side edges of afghan.

Edging: **Rnd 1:** With RS facing, join MC with sc in ch-3 sp at top right corner of afghan, ch 2, sc in same sp, * (ch 1, sc in next sp) 4 times, ch 1, [(sc, ch 2, sc) in next ch-3 sp, (ch 1, sc in next sp) 10 times] 7 times, (sc, ch 2, sc) in next ch-3 sp, (ch 1, sc in next sp) 4 times, ch 1, (sc, ch 2, sc) in next ch-3 sp, (ch 1, sc in next sp) across to next corner ch-3 sp, ch 1 **, (sc, ch 2, sc) in next ch-3 sp, rep from * to ** once more, sl st in first sc.

Rnd 2: Sl st into first sp, ch 4, sc in next ch-1 sp, (ch 1, sc in next ch-1 sp) across to next ch-2 sp, * ch 2, hdc in next ch-2 sp, ch 2, sc in next ch-1 sp, (ch 1, sc in next ch-1 sp) across to next ch-2 sp, rep from * around, ch 2, sl st in 2nd ch of beg ch-4.

Rnd 3: Sl st into first sp, ch 1, (sl st in next sp, ch 1) around, sl st in first sl st. Fasten off.

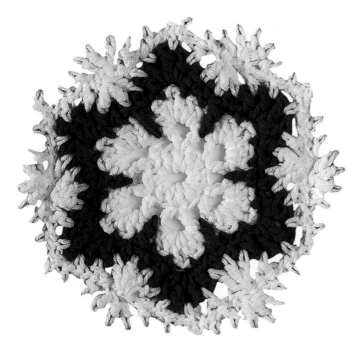

W

Whispers of White

Whispers of White

*Here's a lovely shower gift
that would be just as beautiful in soft pastels.
Scallops and bows add a sweet touch.*

Finished Size

Approximately 33" x 44"

Materials

Lion Brand Jamie Pompadour sportweight yarn
(1.75 oz., 196-yd. skein): 11 White #200
Size F crochet hook or size to obtain gauge
18¼ yards ¼"-wide white satin ribbon
White sewing thread

Gauge

21 dc and 10 rows = 4"

Directions

Afghan: Ch 209 loosely.

Row 1 (WS) (eyelet row): Dc in 8th ch from
hook, (ch 2, sk next 2 ch, dc in next ch) across,
turn = 68 ch-2 sps across.

Row 2 (RS): Ch 3 (for first dc), 3 dc in ea ch-2 sp
across to last sp, 4 dc in last ch-2 sp, turn = 206 dc
across.

Row 3: Ch 3 (for first dc), sk next dc, (dc, ch 1,
dc) in next dc, [sk next 2 dc, (dc, ch 1, dc) in next
dc] across to last 2 dc, sk next dc, dc in last dc, turn =
68 ch-sps across.

Row 4: Ch 3 (for first dc), 3 dc in ea ch-1 sp
across, dc in last dc, turn = 206 dc across.

Rows 5–10: Rep Rows 3 and 4 alternately.

Row 11 (eyelet row): Ch 5 (for first dc and ch 2),
sk next 3 dc, (dc in next dc, ch 2, sk next 2 dc) across
to last dc, dc in last dc, turn = 68 ch-sps across.

Row 12: Rep Row 2.

Rows 13–81: Rep Rows 3–12, ending after last
rep of Row 11. Fasten off after Row 81.

Scallops: *Note:* Scallops are worked 1 at a time across
each short edge of afghan. Each scallop is worked
between ends of 2 eyelet rows.

First Scallop: Row 1: With WS facing and working in ends of rows, join yarn with sl st in st at end of
6th row from corner of afghan (center row bet 2

eyelet rows), ch 1, (sc, ch 5, sc) in same row.

Row 2 (RS): Ch 3 (for first dc), sl st in end of
next row on afghan, turn, 9 dc in ch-5 sp, sl st in end
of next row on afghan = 10 dc.

Row 3: Ch 3 (for first dc), sl st in end of next row
on afghan, ch 1, turn, sk first dc, (dc in next dc, ch 1)
8 times, dc in next dc, sl st in end of next row on
afghan.

Row 4: Ch 3 (for first dc), sl st in end of next row
on afghan, ch 2, turn, sk first dc, (dc in next dc, ch 2)
8 times, dc in next dc, sl st in end of next row on
afghan.

Row 5: Ch 3 (for first dc), sl st in end of next row
on afghan, ch 2, turn, dc in first dc, [(dc, ch 2, dc)
for V-st in next dc] 9 times, sl st in end of next row
on afghan = 10 V-sts. Fasten off.

2nd Scallop: Row 1: With WS facing and working in ends of rows, sk 5 rows from last scallop, join
yarn with sl st in end of next row of afghan, (center
row bet 2 eyelet rows), ch 1, (sc, ch 5, sc) in same
row. Rep Rows 1–5 as for First Scallop. Fasten off.

3rd–8th Scallops: Work as for 2nd Scallop.

Rep to work 8 scallops across rem end of afghan.
Do not fasten off after last scallop.

Edging: With RS facing, sl st in next dc and in next
ch-2 sp, ch 1, sc in same sp, (sc, ch 3, sc) in ea of
next 8 ch-2 sps, sc in next ch-2 sp, * [sc in first ch-2
sp of next Scallop, (sc, ch 3, sc) in ea of next 8 ch-
sps, sc in next ch-2 sp] across Scallops to corner, [sc,
(ch 3, sc) twice] in corner, (sc, ch 3, sc) in ea ch-2 sp
across to next corner, [sc, (ch 3, sc) twice] in corner, rep from * around, end with sl st in first sc.
Fasten off.

Finishing: From ribbon, cut 9 (48") lengths and
14 (16") lengths. With right side facing, weave 1
(48") length through each eyelet row, stitching
ribbon ends to back of afghan. Tie each 16"
length in a bow. Referring to photo, stitch bows to
afghan. Trim streamers as desired.

X

X Marks
the Spot

X Marks the Spot

*Here's another great pattern for beginners.
It's made with very easy squares worked
in rounds of soft chenille yarn.*

Finished Size

Approximately 37" x 48"

Materials

Lion Brand Chenille worsted-weight chenille yarn (1.4 oz., 87-yd. skein): 4 each Silver #149 (A), Denim Blue #111 (B), Brick #134 (C), Midnight Blue #110 (D); 5 Sandstone #155 (E)

Size H crochet hook or size to obtain gauge

Gauge

Square = 4¾"

Directions

Square (make 20 with A, 17 with B, 14 with C, and 12 with D, using E for Rnd 5 on all squares): Ch 5, join with sl st to form a ring.

Rnd 1 (RS): Ch 3 (for first dc), 2 dc in ring, * ch 2, 3 dc in ring, rep from * twice more, ch 2, sl st in 3rd ch of beg ch-3.

Rnd 2: Ch 3 (for first dc), dc in ea of next 2 dc, * (2 dc, ch 2, 2 dc) in next ch-2 sp for corner, dc in ea of next 3 dc, rep from * around, sl st in top of beg ch-3.

Rnds 3 and 4: Ch 3 (for first dc), * dc in ea dc across to next corner ch-2 sp, (2 dc, ch 2, 2 dc) in corner sp, rep from * around, sl st in top of beg ch-3. Fasten off after Rnd 4.

Rnd 5: Join E with sl st in last st, * sc in ea dc across to next corner ch-2 sp, (sc, ch 2, sc) in corner sp, rep from * around, sl st in first sc. Fasten off.

Assembly: Referring to Placement Diagram and working through back loops only, whipstitch squares together.

Edging: **Rnd 1:** With RS facing, join E with sl st in any corner, ch 1, sc in same corner sp, ch 1, * (sk 1 st, sc in next st, ch 1) across to next corner, (sc, ch 1, sc) in corner sp, rep from * around, sl st in first sc. Fasten off.

Rnd 2: Join D with sl st in any corner, ch 3 (for first dc), dc in same corner sp, sk 1 st, * (dc in next ch-1 sp, ch 1, sk next st) across to next corner, (2 dc, ch 1, 2 dc) in corner sp, rep from * around, sl st in top of beg ch-3. Fasten off.

Rnd 3: Join B with sl st in any corner, ch 1, sc in same corner sp, * ch 1, sk 2 corner dc, (sc in next dc, ch 1) across to next corner, sk 2 corner dc, (2 dc, ch 1, 2 dc) in corner sp, rep from * around, sl st in first sc. Fasten off.

Rnd 4: Join D with sl st in any corner, ch 3 (for first dc), dc in same corner sp, * ch 1, sk 2 corner dc, (dc in next ch-1 sp, ch 1) across to next corner, sk 2 corner dc, (2 dc, ch 1, 2 dc) in corner sp, rep from * around, sl st in top of beg ch-3, turn.

Rnd 5: Ch 3, * sc in first ch of ch-3 for picot, sc in next st, sl st in next st, ch 3, rep from * around, sl st in base of beg ch-3. Fasten off.

B	D	A	C	A	D	B
D	A	C	B	C	A	D
A	C	B	A	B	C	A
C	B	A	D	A	B	C
B	A	D	B	D	A	B
C	B	A	D	A	B	C
A	C	B	A	B	C	A
D	A	C	B	C	A	D
B	D	A	C	A	D	B

Placement Diagram

X

Xs and Os

Xs and Os

This afghan is also super for beginners. It's an easy lesson in how to read charts. Then when you're finished stitching, enjoy a game of tic-tac-toe!

Finished Sizes

Afghan: Approximately 43" x 49"
Game Pieces: Approximately 11" x 13"

Materials

Lion Brand Jamie 4 Kids worsted-weight yarn (2 oz., 140-yd. skein): 21 Snow White #100 (A); 2 each Flag Blue #109 (B), Fire Engine Red #113 (C)
Size J crochet hook or size to obtain gauge
Stuffing

Gauge

3 sc = 1"

Directions

Note: To change colors, work last yo of last st in prev color with new color, dropping prev color to WS of work. Do not carry yarn not in use across the row.

Afghan: With A, ch 38, attach B and ch 3, attach another ball of A and ch 38, attach another ball of B and ch 3, attach another ball of A and ch 39 = 121 ch.

Row 1 (RS): With A, sc in 2nd ch from hook and in ea of next 37 ch, (sc in ea of next 3 ch with B, sc in ea of next 38 ch with A) twice, turn = 120 sc across.

Rows 2–50: Ch 1, sc in ea st across, working colors as est in Row 1.

Rows 51–54: Join B in last st of prev row, ch 1, sc in ea st across, turn. Fasten off B after Row 54.

Rep Row 2 for 50 rows.

Rep Rows 51–54.

Rep Row 2 for 50 rows. Fasten off all yarns.

Border: **Rnd 1:** With RS facing, join A with sl st in any corner, * sc evenly across to next corner, 3 sc in corner, rep from * around, sl st in first sc.

continued on page 126

continued from page 125

Rnds 2–6: Ch 1, * sc in ea st to center corner st, 3 sc in corner st, rep from * around, sl st in first sc. Fasten off after last rnd.

Pillow Back (make 8): With A, ch 35.
    Row 1: Sc in 2nd ch from hook and in ea rem ch across, turn = 34 sc across.
    Rows 2–46: Ch 1, sc in ea st across, turn. Fasten off after Row 46.

Pillow Front (make 4 with X and 4 with O): With A, ch 35.
    Row 1 (RS): Sc in 2nd ch from hook and in ea rem ch across, turn = 34 sc across.

Rows 2–46: Ch 1, work in sc, changing colors according to charts. Read chart from right to left on odd-numbered rows (RS) and left to right on even-numbered rows (WS). Fasten off after Row 46.

Pillow Assembly: With wrong sides facing and edges aligned, hold pillow front and back together, join A with sl st in any corner, working through both layers, (sc evenly to next corner, 3 sc in corner) 3 times, stuff pillow lightly, sc evenly across rem edge, sl st in first sc. Repeat to assemble each pillow.

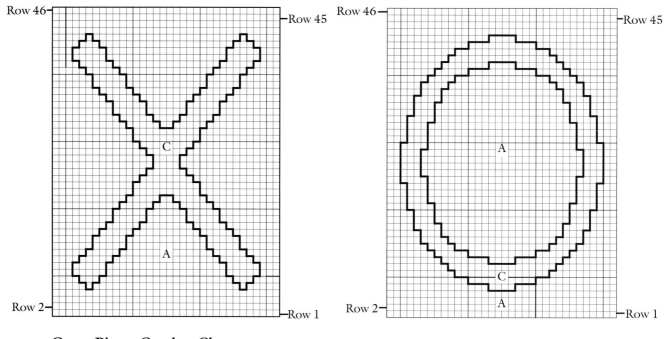

Game Pieces Crochet Charts

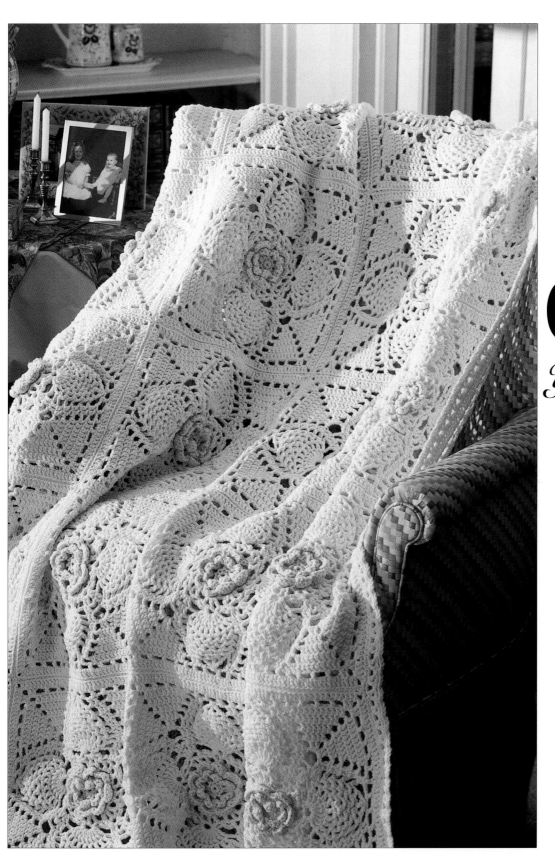

Y
Yesterday

Yesterday

Delicate flowers like these will always be in style. This lovely and challenging pattern requires experience in crochet.

Finished Size

Approximately 52" x 78"

Materials

Lion Brand Keepsake Sayelle* worsted-weight yarn (6 oz., 312-yd. skein): 10 Cream #098 (MC), 2 Peach #184 (CC)

Size H crochet hook or size to obtain gauge

Gauge

Square = 13"

Directions

Square (make 24): **Rnd 1** (RS): With CC, ch 2, 8 sc in 2nd ch from hook, sl st in first sc to form a ring = 8 sc around.

Rnd 2: Ch 1, sc in same st, ch 3, (sc in next sc, ch 3) around, sl st in first sc = 8 ch-3 sps around.

Rnd 3: Sl st into next ch-3 sp, ch 1, (sc, 3 dc, sc) in ea ch-3 sp around, sl st in first sc = 8 petals.

Rnd 4: Working behind petals, sc around post of first rnd-2 sc, ch 4, (sc around post of next rnd-2 sc, ch 4) around, sl st in first sc = 8 lps around.

Rnd 5: Sl st into next lp, ch 1, (sc, 5 dc, sc) in ea ch-4 lp around, sl st in first sc = 8 petals.

Rnd 6: Working behind petals, sc around post of first rnd-4 sc, ch 5, (sc around post of next rnd-4 sc, ch 5) around, sl st in first sc = 8 lps around. Fasten off.

Rnd 7: With RS facing, join MC with sl st in any lp, ch 5 (for first dc and ch 2), (dc, ch 2) twice in same lp, (dc, ch 2) 3 times in ea lp around, sl st in 3rd ch of beg ch-5 = 24 ch-2 sps around.

Rnd 8: Sl st into next ch-2 sp, ch 1, sc in same sp, ch 3, (sc in next ch-2 sp, ch 3) around, sl st in first sc = 24 ch-3 sps around.

Rnd 9: Sl st into next ch-3 sp, ch 3 (for first dc), (dc, ch 3, 2 dc) in same sp, * ch 3, sk next 2 ch-3 sps, 9 tr in next ch-3 sp, ch 3, sk next 2 ch-3 sps **, (2 dc, ch 3, 2 dc) in next ch-3 sp, rep from * around, ending last rep at **, sl st in top of beg ch-3.

Rnd 10: Ch 3 (for first dc), dc in next dc, ch 3, dc in ea of next 2 dc, ch 3, * dc in next tr, (ch 1, dc in next tr) 8 times, ch 3 **, (dc in ea of next 2 dc, ch 3) twice, rep from * around, ending last rep at **, sl st in top of beg ch-3.

Rnd 11: Ch 3 (for first dc), dc in next dc, * ch 5, dc in ea of next 2 dc, ch 3, sc in next ch-1 sp, (ch 3, sc in next ch-3 sp) 7 times, ch 3 **, dc in ea of next 2 dc, rep from * around, ending last rep at **, sl st in top of beg ch-3.

Rnd 12: Ch 3 (for first dc), dc in next dc, ch 3, * (2 dc, ch 3) twice in next ch-5 sp, dc in ea of next 2 dc, ch 3, sk next ch-3 sp, sc in next ch-3 sp, (ch 3, sc in next ch-3 sp) 6 times, ch 3 **, dc in ea of next 2 dc, ch 3, rep from * around, ending last rep at **, sl st in top of beg ch-3.

Rnd 13: Ch 3 (for first dc), dc in next dc, ch 3, dc in next ch-3 sp, * dc in ea of next 2 dc, (dc, ch 3, dc) in next ch-3 sp, dc in ea of next 2 dc, dc in next ch-3 sp, ch 3, dc in ea of next 2 dc, ch 3, sk next ch-3 sp, sc in next ch-3 sp, (ch 3, sc in next ch-3 sp) 5 times, ch 3 **, dc in ea of next 2 dc, ch 3, dc in next ch-3 sp, rep from * around, ending last rep at **, sl st in top of beg ch-3.

Rnd 14: Ch 3 (for first dc), dc in next dc, * ch 3, dc in next ch-3 sp, dc in ea of next 4 dc, (dc, ch 3, dc) in next ch-3 sp, dc in ea of next 4 dc, dc in next ch-3 sp, ch 3, dc in ea of next 2 dc, ch 3, sk next ch-3 sp, sc in next ch-3 sp, (ch 3, sc in next ch-3 sp) 4 times, ch 3 **, dc in ea of next 2 dc, rep from * around, ending last rep at **, sl st in top of beg ch-3.

Rnd 15: Ch 3 (for first dc), dc in next dc, * ch 3, dc in next ch-3 sp, dc in ea of next 6 dc, (dc, ch 3, dc) in next ch-3 sp, dc in ea of next 6 dc, dc in next ch-3 sp, ch 3, dc in ea of next 2 dc, ch 3, sk next ch-3 sp, sc in next ch-3 sp, (ch 3, sc in next ch-3 sp) 3 times, ch 3 **, dc in ea of next 2 dc, rep from * around, ending last rep at **, sl st in top of beg ch-3.

Rnd 16: Ch 6 (for first dc and ch 3), * dc in next ch-3 sp, dc in ea of next 8 dc, (dc, ch 3, dc) in next ch-3 sp, dc in ea of next 8 dc, dc in next ch-3 sp, ch 3, sk next dc, dc in next dc, dc in next ch-3 sp, ch 3, keeping last lp of ea st on hook, tr in ea of next 3 ch-3 sps, yo and pull through all 4 lps on hook (dec made over 3 sps), ch 3, dc in next ch-3 sp **, dc in next dc, ch 3, rep from * around, ending last rep at **, sl st in 3rd ch of beg ch-6.

Rnd 17: Ch 5 (for first dc and ch 2), dc in next ch-3 sp, * ch 2, sk next dc, dc in next dc, (ch 2, sk next 2 dc, dc in next dc) twice, ch 2, (2 dc, ch 3, 2 dc) in next ch-3 sp, (ch 2, sk next 2 dc, dc in next dc) 3 times, ch 2, dc in next ch-3 sp, ch 2, dc in next dc, (ch 2, dc in next ch-3 sp) twice, ch 2, sk next dc **, dc in next dc, ch 2, dc in next ch-3 sp, rep from * around, ending last rep at **, sl st in 3rd ch of beg ch-5 = 56 sps around.

Rnd 18: Ch 3 (for first dc), 2 dc in next ch-2 sp, (dc in next dc, 2 dc in next ch-2 sp) 4 times, * dc in ea of next 2 dc, (2 dc, ch 3, 2 dc) in next ch-3 sp, dc in ea of next 2 dc, 2 dc in next ch-2 sp **, (dc in next dc, 2 dc in next ch-2 sp) 12 times, rep from * around, ending last rep at **, (dc in next dc, 2 dc in next ch-2 sp) 7 times, sl st in top of beg ch-3. Fasten off.

Assembly: Afghan is 4 squares wide and 6 squares long. With right sides facing and working in back loops only, whipstitch squares together.

Edging: **Rnd 1:** With RS facing and afghan turned to work across 1 short edge, join MC with sl st in corner ch-3 sp, ch 1, * 3 sc in corner sp, sc in ea of next 46 dc, (sc in ch-3 sp before joining, sc in joining, sc in ch-3 sp after joining, sc in ea of next 46 dc) across to next corner ch-3 sp, rep from * around, sl st in first sc = 980 sc around.

Rnd 2: Ch 4 (for first dc and ch 1), dc in same st, (dc, ch 1, dc for V-st) in ea of next 2 sc, sk next sc, (V-st in next sc, sk next 2 sc) across to next corner, * V-st in ea of next 3 sc, sk next 3 sc, (V-st in next sc, sk next 2 sc) across to next corner **, V-st in ea of next 3 sc, sk next sc, (V-st in next sc, sk next 2 sc) across to next corner, rep from * to **, sl st in 3rd ch of beg ch-4 = 332 V-sts around.

Rnd 3: Sl st in next ch-1 sp, sl st in next dc, sl st in sp before next dc, ch 1, sc in same sp, ch 3, (sk next V-st, sc in sp before next V-st, ch 3) around, sl st in first sc. Fasten off.

Year-round Comfort

Year-round Comfort

Pretty puff stitches worked into rows of diamonds give the effect of a fisherman's pullover—a classic that is in fashion year-round.

Finished Size

Approximately 48" x 60"

Materials

Lion Brand Jiffy chunky-weight mohair-look yarn (3 oz., 135-yd. ball): 20 Fisherman #99
Size J crochet hook or size to obtain gauge

Gauge

10 sc and 13 rows = 4"

Pattern Stitch

Puff st: (Yo and pull up a lp) 5 times in st 2 rows below next st, yo and pull through all lps on hook to complete puff st. Sk 1 st behind ea puff st.

Directions

Afghan: **Row 1:** Ch 124 loosely, sc in 2nd ch from hook and in ea rem ch across, turn = 123 sc across.

Row 2 and all even-numbered rows (RS): Ch 1, sc in ea st across, turn.

Row 3: Ch 1, sc in first sc, * work puff st, sk 1 st behind puff st, sc in ea of next 11 sc, rep from * across, end with puff st, sk 1 st behind puff st, sc in last sc, turn.

Row 5: Ch 1, sc in ea of first 2 sc, * work puff st, sk 1 st behind puff st, sc in ea of next 9 sc, puff st, sk 1 st behind puff st, sc in next sc, rep from * across, end with sc in last sc, turn.

Row 7: Ch 1, sc in ea of first 3 sc, * work puff st, sk 1 st behind puff st, sc in ea of next 7 sc, puff st, sk 1 st behind puff st, sc in ea of next 3 sc, rep from * across, turn.

Row 9: Ch 1, sc in ea of first 4 sc, * work puff st, sk 1 st behind puff st, sc in ea of next 5 sc, rep from * across, end with puff st, sk 1 st behind puff st, sc in ea of last 4 sc, turn.

Row 11: Ch 1, sc in ea of first 5 sc, * work puff st, sk 1 st behind puff st, sc in ea of next 3 sc, puff st, sk 1 st behind puff st, sc in ea of next 7 sc, rep from * across, end with sc in ea of last 5 sc, turn.

Row 13: Ch 1, sc in ea of first 6 sc, * work puff st, sk 1 st behind puff st, sc in next sc, puff st, sk 1 st behind puff st, sc in ea of next 9 sc, rep from * across, end with sc in ea of last 6 sc, turn.

Row 15: Ch 1, sc in ea of first 7 sc, * work puff st, sk 1 st behind puff st, sc in ea of next 11 sc, rep from * across, end with puff st, sk 1 st behind puff st, sc in ea of last 7 sc.

Row 17: Rep Row 13.
Row 19: Rep Row 11.
Row 21: Rep Row 9.
Row 23: Rep Row 7.
Row 25: Rep Row 5.
Rows 26–195: Rep Rows 2–25 for pat. Do not fasten off.

Border: With RS facing, ch 1, * sc evenly across to next corner, 3 sc in corner, rep from * around, sl st in first sc. Fasten off.

Zipper
Tape

Zipper Tape

Super-easy, super-quick, you can zip through this afghan in no time at all. And because it's made in simple strips, it's a portable project.

Finished Size

Approximately 45" x 64"

Materials

Lion Brand Keepsake Sayelle* worsted-weight yarn (6 oz., 312-yd. skein): 5 Marine Blue #110 (MC), 3 Silver #149 (CC)

Sizes G and H crochet hooks or sizes to obtain gauge

Gauge

Shell Strip = 2" wide, 10 rows = 8" with size H hook

10 (3-dc) grps (edging in pat) = 8" with size G hook

Pattern Stitch

Double triple (dtr): (Yo 3 times, insert hook where indicated and pull up a lp, yo and pull through 2 lps on hook) 4 times.

Directions

Shell Strip (make 14): With size H hook and MC, ch 6, join with sl st to form a ring.

Row 1 (RS): Ch 3 (for first dc), (2 dc, ch 2, 3 dc) in ring, turn.

Rows 2–80: Ch 3 (for first dc), (3 dc, ch 2, 3 dc) in ch-2 sp, dc in top of tch = center shells made. Fasten off after last row.

Edging: With RS of Shell Strip facing and size G hook, join CC with sl st in beg ring, ch 5 (for first dtr), 14 dtr in same ring, working down side of strip, work 3 dc in ch-3 sp at end of ea row across to end of strip, work 15 dtr in ch-2 sp at end of strip, working down side of strip, work 3 dc in ch-3 sp at end of ea row across to end of strip, sl st in top of beg ch-5 = 79 (3-dc) grps on ea side of strip. Fasten off.

Joining: With RS facing and size G hook, join MC with sl st in first dc at top of First Shell Strip, ch 1, sc in same dc, ch 2, sc in corresponding first dc at top of 2nd Shell Strip, * ch 2, sk next dc on First Shell Strip, sc in next dc on First Shell Strip, ch 2, sk next dc on 2nd Shell Strip, sc in next dc on 2nd Shell Strip, rep from * across. Fasten off. Rep to join rem strips.

Border: With RS facing and using size G hook, join MC with sl st in any st, ch 1, working in crab st (reverse sc) from left to right (instead of right to left), sc in ea st around, sl st in first sc. Fasten off.

Z

Zebra Garden

Zebra Garden

Choose any two-color combination for this sensational sampler.

Finished Size

Approximately 46" x 62"

Materials

Lion Brand Keepsake Sayelle* worsted-weight yarn (6 oz., 312-yd. skein): 4 White #100 (MC), 5 Black #153 (CC)

Size J crochet hook or size to obtain gauge

Gauge

Block = 8" square

Directions

Popcorn Block (make 9): With MC, ch 4, join with sl st to form a ring.

Rnd 1 (RS): Ch 3 (for first dc), 15 dc in ring, sl st in top of beg ch-3 = 16 dc around.

Rnd 2: Ch 4 (for first dc and ch 1), * dc in next dc, ch 1, rep from * around, sl st in 3rd ch of beg ch-4 = 16 ch-1 sps around. Draw CC through lp on hook and fasten off MC.

Rnd 3: With CC, ch 3 (for first dc), 4 dc in first ch-1 sp, drop last lp from hook, insert hook from front to back through top of beg ch-3, pick up dropped lp and draw through (beg popcorn made), ch 2, * 5 dc in next ch-1 sp, drop last lp from hook, insert hook from front to back through top of first dc of 5-dc grp, pick up dropped lp and draw through (popcorn made), ch 2, rep from * around, sl st in top of beg popcorn = 16 popcorns around. Change to MC and fasten off CC.

Rnd 4: With MC, ch 3 (for first dc), 2 dc in last ch-2 sp of prev rnd, * 3 dc in ea of next 3 sps, (3 dc, ch 2, 3 dc) in next sp for corner, rep from * around, end with 3 dc in same sp as beg ch-3, ch 2, sl st in top of beg ch-3 = 60 dc around. Change to CC and fasten off MC.

Rnd 5: With CC, ch 3 (for first dc), * dc in ea dc to next corner sp, 3 dc in corner ch-2 sp, rep from * around, sl st in top of beg ch-3 = 72 dc around. Change to MC and fasten off CC.

continued on page 136

continued from page 135

Rnd 6: With MC, ch 3 (for first dc), * dc in ea dc to center corner st, 3 dc in corner st, rep from * around, sl st in top of beg ch-3 = 80 dc around. Fasten off.

Granny Square Block (make 9): With MC, ch 4, join with sl st to form a ring.

Rnd 1: Ch 3 (for first dc), 2 dc in ring, * ch 3, 3 dc in ring, rep from * twice more, ch 3, sl st in top of beg ch-3 = 4 (3-dc) grps around. Fasten off MC.

Rnd 2: Join CC with sl st in any ch-3 sp, ch 3 (for first dc), 2 dc in same sp, * ch 2, (3 dc, ch 3, 3 dc) in next ch-3 sp (for corner), rep from * twice more, ch 2, 3 dc in same sp as beg ch-3, ch 3, sl st in top of beg ch-3 = 8 (3-dc) grps around. Fasten off CC.

Rnd 3: Join MC with sl st in any corner ch-3 sp, ch 3 (for first dc), 2 dc in same sp, * ch 2, 3 dc in next ch-2 sp, ch 2, (3 dc, ch 3, 3 dc) in next ch-3 sp for corner, rep from * around, end with ch 2, 3 dc in beg corner sp, ch 3, sl st in top of beg ch-3 = 12 (3-dc) grps around. Fasten off MC.

Rnd 4: Join CC with sl st in any corner ch-3 sp, ch 3 (for first dc), 2 dc in same sp, * ch 2, (3 dc, ch 2) in ea ch-2 sp to next corner sp, (3 dc, ch 3, 3 dc) in corner ch-3 sp, rep from * around, end with ch 2, 3 dc in beg corner sp, ch 3, sl st in top of beg ch-3 = 16 (3-dc) grps around. Fasten off CC.

Rnd 5: Join MC with sl st in any corner ch-3 sp, rep Rnd 4 = 20 (3-dc) grps around. Fasten off MC.

Rnd 6: Join CC with sl st in any corner ch-3 sp, rep Rnd 4 = 24 (3-dc) grps around. Fasten off.

Wheel Block (make 8): With MC, ch 8, join with sl st to form a ring.

Rnd 1: Ch 3 (for first dc), 15 dc in ring, sl st in top of beg ch-3 = 16 dc around.

Rnd 2: Ch 5 (for first dc and ch 2), (dc in next dc, ch 2) 15 times, sl st in 3rd ch of beg ch-5 = 16 ch-2 sps around.

Rnd 3: Ch 3 (for first dc), 2 dc in first sp, ch 1, (3 dc, ch 1) in ea sp around, sl st in top of beg ch-3 = 16 ch-1 sps around. Fasten off MC.

Rnd 4: Join CC with sl st in any ch-1 sp, sc in same sp, * (ch 3, sc in next ch-1 sp) 3 times, ch 6 for corner lp, sc in next sp, rep from * around, end with

ch 6, sl st in first sc = 3 ch-3 lps bet corner ch-6 lps.

Rnd 5: Ch 3 (for first dc), 2 dc in first ch-3 sp, * 3 dc in ea ch-3 sp to next corner lp, (5 dc, ch 2, 5 dc) in corner ch-6 lp, rep from * around, sl st in top of beg ch-3 = 76 dc around.

Rnd 6: Ch 3 (for first dc), * dc in ea dc to next corner sp, (dc, tr, dc) in corner ch-2 sp, rep from * around, sl st in top of beg ch-3 = 21 dc bet corner tr. Fasten off.

Box Block (make 9): With CC, ch 6, join with sl st to form a ring.

Rnd 1: Ch 3 (for first dc), 2 dc in ring, ch 1, (3 dc in ring, ch 1) 3 times, sl st in top of beg ch-3 = 12 dc around.

Rnd 2: Ch 3 (for first dc), dc in ea of next 2 dc, * (2 dc, ch 1, 2 dc) in next ch-1 sp for corner, dc in ea of next 3 dc, rep from * around, end with (2 dc, ch 1, 2 dc) in last ch-1 sp, sl st in top of beg ch-3 = 28 dc around. Fasten off CC.

Rnd 3: Join MC with sl st in same st as sl st, ch 3 (for first dc), * dc in ea dc to next corner sp, (2 dc, ch 1, 2 dc) in corner ch-1 sp, rep from * around, end with dc in ea dc to beg ch-3, sl st in top of beg ch-3 = 44 dc around. Fasten off MC.

Rnds 4 and 5: Join CC with sl st in same st as sl st, rep Rnd 3 = 76 dc around after Rnd 5. Fasten off CC after Rnd 5.

Rnd 6: Join MC with sl st in same st as sl st, rep Rnd 3 = 92 dc around. Fasten off.

Assembly: Whipstitch blocks together as desired.

Border: **Rnd 1:** With RS facing, join MC with sl st in any corner, ch 3 (for first dc), * dc in ea st to next corner, 3 dc in corner, rep from * around, sl st in top of beg ch-3. Fasten off MC.

Rnd 2: Join CC with sl st in any center corner st, ch 3 (for first dc), * dc in ea st to next center corner st, 3 dc in corner st, rep from * around, sl st in top of beg ch-3. Fasten off CC.

Rnds 3 and 4: Join MC with sl st in any center corner st, rep Rnd 2. Fasten off MC after Rnd 4.

Rnd 5: Join CC with sl st in any center corner st, rep Rnd 2. Fasten off.

General Directions

CROCHET ABBREVIATIONS

beg	begin(ning)
bet	between
bk lp(s)	back loop(s)
ch	chain(s)
ch-	refers to chain previously made
cl	cluster(s)
cont	continu(e) (ing)
dc	double crochet
dec	decrease(s) (d) (ing)
dtr	double triple crochet
ea	each
est	established
foll	follow(s) (ing)
ft lp(s)	front loop(s)
grp(s)	group(s)
hdc	half double crochet
inc	increase(s) (d) (ing)
lp(s)	loop(s)
pat(s)	pattern(s)
prev	previous
rem	remain(s) (ing)
rep	repeat(s)
rnd(s)	round(s)
RS	right side
sc	single crochet
sk	skip(ped)
sl st	slip stitch
sp(s)	space(s)
st(s)	stitch(es)
tch	turning chain
tog	together
tr	triple crochet
WS	wrong side
yo	yarn over

Repeat whatever follows * as indicated. "Rep from * 3 times more" means to work four times in all.

Work directions given in parentheses and brackets the number of times specified or in the place specified.

GAUGE

Before beginning a project, work a 4"-square gauge swatch using the recommended size hook. Count and compare the number of stitches per inch in the swatch with the specified gauge. If you have fewer stitches in your swatch, try a smaller hook; if you have more stitches, try a larger hook.

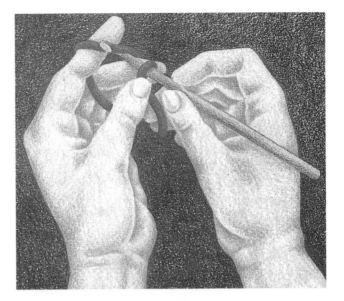

WORKING TOGETHER

Hold the hook as you would a pencil (shown above) or a piece of chalk. Weave the yarn through the fingers of your left hand to control the amount of yarn fed into the work and to provide tension. Once work has begun, the thumb and the middle finger of the left hand come into play, pressing together to hold the stitches just made.

SLIP STITCH DIAGRAM

Above a slip stitch (sl st) is used to join a ring. Taking care not to twist the chain, insert the hook into the first chain made, yarn over, and pull through the chain and the loop on the hook (sl st made). The sl st can also be used to join finished pieces (see page 140) or to move across a group of stitches without adding height to the work.

SLIP KNOT DIAGRAM

Loop the yarn around and let the loose end of the yarn fall behind the loop to form a pretzel shape as shown. Insert the hook (**A**) and pull both ends to close the knot (**B**).

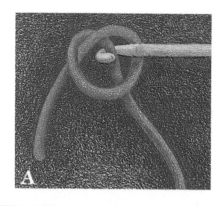

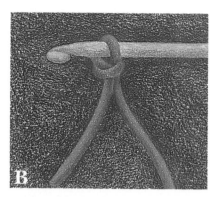

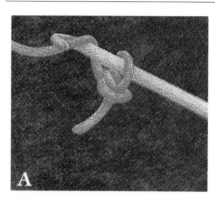

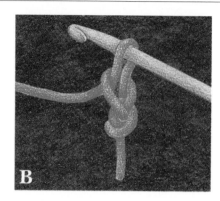

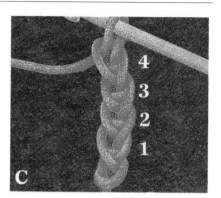

CHAIN STITCH DIAGRAM

A. Place a slip knot on your hook. With hands in the position shown above and with the thumb and the middle finger of your left hand holding the yarn end, wrap the yarn up and over the hook (from back to front). This movement is called a "yarn over" (yo) and is basic to every crochet stitch.

B. Use the hook to pull the yarn through the loop (lp) already on the hook. The combination of yo and pulling the yarn through the lp makes 1 chain stitch (ch).

C. Repeat until the ch is the desired length, trying to keep the movements even and relaxed, and all the ch stitches (sts) the same size. Hold the ch near the working area to keep it from twisting. Count sts as shown above. (Do not count the lp on the hook or the slip knot.)

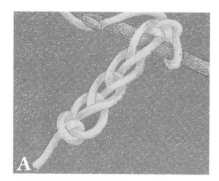

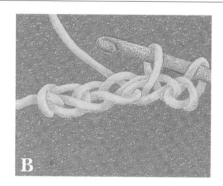

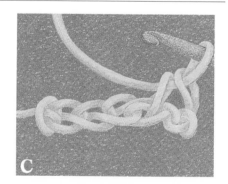

SINGLE CROCHET DIAGRAM

A. Insert hook under top 2 lps of 2nd ch from hook and yo. (Always work sts through top 2 lps unless directions specify otherwise.)

B. Pull yarn through ch (2 lps on hook).

C. Yo and pull yarn through 2 lps on hook. One single crochet (sc) made.

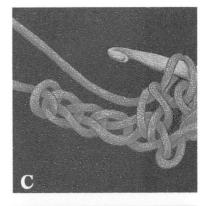

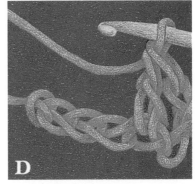

DOUBLE CROCHET DIAGRAM

A. Yo, insert hook into 4th ch from hook, and yo.

B. Pull yarn through ch (3 lps on hook).

C. Yo and pull through 2 lps on hook (2 lps remaining).

(*Note:* When directions say "keeping last lp of ea st on hook," this means to work the specified st to the final yo. This is done to make a cluster or to work a decrease.)

D. Yo and pull through 2 remaining (rem) lps. One double crochet (dc) made.

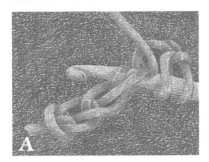

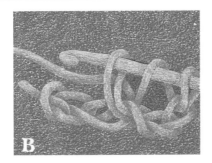

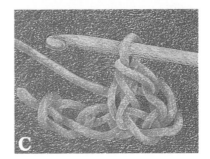

HALF DOUBLE CROCHET DIAGRAM

A. Yo and insert hook into 3rd ch from hook.

B. Yo and pull through ch (3 lps on hook).

C. Yo and pull yarn through all 3 lps on hook. One half double crochet (hdc) made.

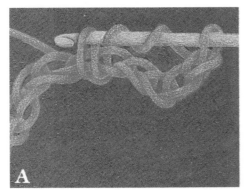

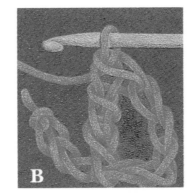

TRIPLE CROCHET DIAGRAM

A. Yo twice, insert hook into 5th ch from hook. Yo and pull through ch (4 lps on hook).

B. Yo and pull through 2 lps on hook (3 lps rem). Yo and pull through 2 lps on hook (2 lps rem). Yo and pull through 2 lps on hook. One triple crochet (tr) made.

ASSEMBLY

To assemble crocheted pieces when making an afghan, use a yarn needle to whipstitch (A) or a crochet hook to slip stitch (B) the pieces together. Pieces can also be joined using single crochet stitches, but this makes a heavier seam.

When making squares or other pieces to be stitched together, leave a 20" tail of yarn when fastening off. This yarn tail can then be used to stitch the pieces together. Also be sure all stitches and rows of the squares or the strips are aligned and running in the same direction.

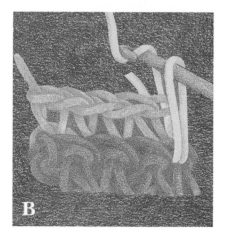

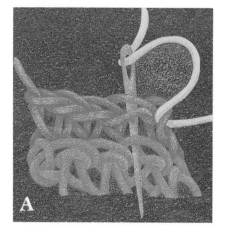

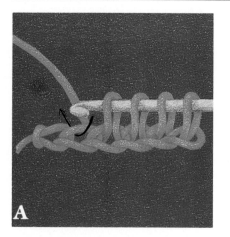

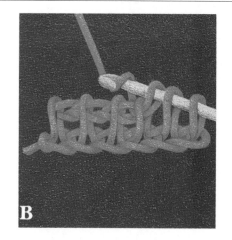

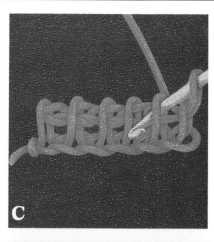

AFGHAN STITCH DIAGRAM

A. *Row 1: Step 1:* Keeping all lps on hook, pull up a lp through top lp only, in 2nd ch from hook and in each ch across = same number of lps and ch. Do not turn.

B. *Step 2:* Yo and pull through first lp on hook, * yo and pull through 2 lps on hook, rep from * across (1 lp rem on hook for first lp of next row). Do not turn.

C. *Row 2: Step 1:* Keeping all lps on hook, pull up a lp from under 2nd vertical bar, * pull up a lp from under next vertical bar, rep from * across. Do not turn. *Step 2:* Rep Step 2 of Row 1.

Rep both steps of Row 2 for the required number of rows. Fasten off after last row by working sl st in each bar across.

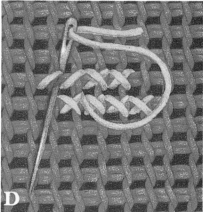

D. When the fabric is finished, it is a perfect grid for cross-stitch.

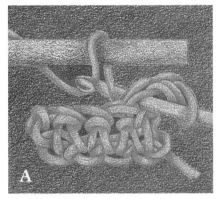

Loop Stitch

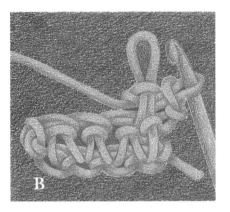

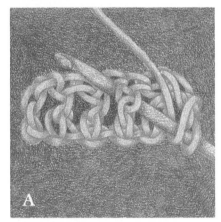

Front Post Double Crochet

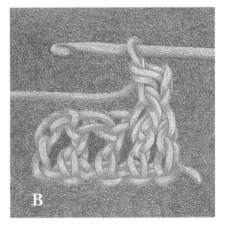

TEXTURE STITCHES

By varying the placement of the basic stitches, you can add texture to your work. Here are two simple variations for use with sc and dc sts. To use these stitches in an afghan, see *Little Lambs* on page 66 or *Pretty Baskets* on page 88.

To make a loop stitch (lp st), with the wrong side of the work facing, insert the hook in the specified st. Wrap yarn over a ruler or your index finger to form a 1"-high loop. Pick up the bottom strand of yarn with the hook and pull through st, keeping lp taut (**A**). Yo and pull through both lps on the hook to complete st as an sc (**B**).

To work a Front Post dc (FPdc), yo and insert the hook from the front to the back around the post of st on the previous row (**A**). Complete dc st as usual (**B**). Working a back post dc is done in the same manner, except you insert the hook from the back to the front around the post.

Fringe

FRINGE AND TASSELS

Finishing touches are an important part of your work. To make a simple fringe, cut the number of yarn lengths specified in the directions. Insert the hook through 1 st at the edge of the afghan and fold the yarn lengths in half over the hook (**A**). Pull the folded yarn halfway through the st (**B**). Pull the yarn ends through the loop (**C**) and pull tight (**D**).

For a tassel, wrap yarn around a piece of cardboard as specified in the directions. At 1 end, slip a 5" yarn length under the loops and knot. Cut the loops at the other end (**A**). Loop and tightly wrap a 36" yarn length around the tassel (**B**). Secure the yarn ends and tuck them into the tassel.

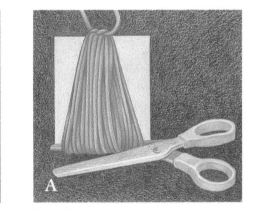

Tassel

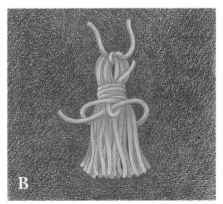

Contributors

DESIGNERS

Mary Lamb Becker, *American Beauty*
Marion Graham, *Buttered Popcorn*
Cathy Grivnow, *Lovely Poppies*
Anne Halliday, *Granny's Delight, Merry Christmas Wreaths, Perfectly Pink,*
　　Winter Wonderland
Jeneel Johnson, *Zipper Tape*
Shala Suzanne Johnson, *Radio Waves*
Terry Kimbrough, *Whispers of White, Yesterday*
Linda Luder, *Under the Mulberry Tree*
Cheryl Kay Meadors, *Blanket Buddies*
Carole Prior, *August Morning*
Mary Ann Sipes, *Stained Glass*
Carole Rutter Tippett, *Pretty Baskets, Quick and Cozy*
Vanna White, *Vanna's Choice*

LION BRAND YARN DESIGNS

Can I Buy a Vowel?, Cat's Meow, Daisy Patchwork, Dreamweaver, Elegant Rose, Edelweiss, Football Fever, Fish in the Sea, Giggles and Squiggles, Hudson's Bay Memory, Hooked on Checkers, Ice Crystals, I Wish I Could Fly, Jigsaw Fun, Jewels of the Nile, Kiss Me Quick, King of the Jungle, Little Lambs, Mix and Match, Nursery Sampler, Night Blooms, Ode to Santa Fe, October Afternoon, Quiet Moments, Rainbow Treasure, Shooting Marbles, Tea Time, Tickle the Ivories, Utter Elegance, Victorian Lace, X Marks the Spot, Xs and Os, Year-round Comfort, Zebra Garden

PHOTOGRAPHERS

Photographs were taken by **John O'Hagan,** except the following:
Ralph Anderson, cover, 1, 3, 6, 7, 8, 28, 38, 46, 50, 56, 58, 70–71, 74, 85, 92, 108, 112,
　　130, 134–135, 144

SPECIAL THANKS

Louise Hewlett
Lori Jean Karluk
Linens by Loraine
The London Knitting Company
Isabel Lyle

Mary Ramey
Lew Robertson
Jeffie Self
Josie Thrasher
Carol Tipton

Lion Brand® Yarns

Jiffy® (Art. No. 450)
100% Monsanto Acrylic
Chunky-weight mohair-look yarn
Solid color balls: 3 oz./85 gr., 135-yd.
Multicolor balls: 2.5 oz./70.88 gr., 115-yd.

Jiffy® Chunky (Art. No. 470)
100% Monsanto Wintuk*
Bulky-weight yarn
Ball: 3 oz./85 gr., 120-yd.

Keepsake® Sayelle* (Art. No. 610)
100% Monsanto Acrylic
Worsted-weight yarn
Solid color skein: 6 oz./170 gr., 312-yd.
Multicolor skein: 5 oz./141 gr., 260-yd.

Jamie® 4 Kids (Art. No. 860)
100% Monsanto Wintuk*
Worsted-weight yarn
Skein: 2 oz./56.7 gr., 140-yd.

Jamie® Pompadour (Art. No. 890)
85% Sayelle* with a 15% rayon wrap
Sportweight yarn
Solid color skein: 1.75 oz./50 gr., 196-yd.
Print skein: 1.5 oz./42.5 gr., 170-yd.

Lion® Chenille (Art. No. 710)
100% Acrylic
Worsted-weight chenille-type yarn
Skein: 1.4 oz./40 gr., 87-yd.

(* = Monsanto certification mark)

LAUNDERING DIRECTIONS

Jiffy, **Jiffy Chunky, Jamie 4 Kids, Jamie Pompodour,** and **Keepsake Sayelle:** Machine-wash using warm water and mild detergent. Machine-dry on low setting.

Chenille: Hand-wash using warm water and mild detergent. Rinse in cold water. Roll item in towels to remove excess water. Lay flat to dry.

To order the Lion Brand Yarns used to create all the afghans in this book, please call 1-800-258-YARN (9276). Lion Brand Yarns are also available at leading stores across the country.

Vanna White

Hostess of the game show "Wheel of Fortune" since 1982, Vanna White has become one of the most popular figures in American television. Her appearance each weekday is a welcome event in homes from coast to coast. Born in Myrtle Beach, South Carolina, the former model has built an entertainment career that includes a best-selling diet video, an autobiography, and countless appearances on magazine covers and talk shows. Vanna also cherishes her roles as wife of George Santopietro and new mother to baby Nicholas.

In spite of her busy schedule—or perhaps because of it—Vanna finds it soothing and rewarding to make the pleasant pastime of crochet part of her daily routine. In *Vanna's Afghans A to Z: 52 Crochet Favorites,* she encourages friends and fans to get in on the fun.